AF556248

UNORGANISED WOMEN LABOUR IN INDIA

UNORGANISED WOMEN LABOUR IN INDIA

Edited by
S.N. TRIPATHY

1996
DISCOVERY PUBLISHING HOUSE
NEW DELHI - 110002 (INDIA)

First Published - 1996

ISBN 81-7141-325-0

Published by :

Discovery Publishing House
4831/24, Ansari Road, Darya Ganj,
New Delhi - 110 002 (INDIA)
Phone : 327 9245
Fax. : 91-11-3253475

Laser Typesetting by :

Debug Computer Services
Delhi.

Printed at :

Tarun Offset Printers, Maujpur
Delhi-53, Phone : 2260794

Contents

Preface VII

1. Plight of Unorganised Women Workers 1
Dr. I. Satyasundaram

2. Unorganised Women Workers : Problems and Prospects 15
Dr. Nancy David

3. Rural Women and Development 27
Dr. Hemalatha Prasad

4. Women in Development 42
Avaya Kesari Parichha Patnaik

5. Tribal Women and their Participation in Developmental Activities 53
S.K. Sahu

6. Occupation and Educational Change of Tribal Women of Assam : A Case Study 64
Dr. Pranay Jyoti Goswami

7. A Case Study of Women Potters in Dakshina Kannada District of Karnataka 79
A.V. Yadappanavar

8. Problems of Rural Women Workers in Readymade Garments : Andhra Pradesh and Karnataka 87
Dr. A. Mohiuddin & Dr. Vikaram Singh

9. Women Labour in Construction Sector : A Study in Orissa 105
Dr. S.N. Tripathy

10. Socio-economic Profile of Fisherwomen Community of Krushnaprasad Block (Orissa) 123
Dr. S.N. Tripathy & P.K. Patnaik

11. Socio-economic Issues and Women Legislators of Orissa : During British Period (1936-1947) 141
Dr. V. Rajendra Raju

Preface

Women constitute half of the world population, do two-thirds of the world's income and own less than a hundredth of the World's property. In India, 90 per cent of women are employed in unorganised sector, without fair wage and standard of living. Domestic women labourers do get a paltry sum for the unpleasant work they perform. Some of them are exploited economically as well as physically.

With the growth of industrialisation and urbanisation, landless labourers in the absence of assured source of employment in rural areas, migrate to urban areas in search of employment. In urban areas, women are generally employed in informal sectors like weaving, handicraft, tailoring, sale of fish and construction activities.

Working women, despite their economic independence, are not truly independent. Neither do they have any control over their own income nor they are allowed to take vital decisions of their life. They sacrifice their right for preserving family place and adjust to all situations.

Unorganised women labourers are outside the reach of most laws which seek to protect their security and living conditions. They are exposed to various exploitations, discriminations and various diseases.

In the Forth International Conference held at Beijing, it has been conceived that the key to social progress lies with the development of women. Two important standards like the gender related development index and gender empowerment measure have been evolved in order to measure human development. Of course, the debt burden has forced many developing countries including India, to undertake structural adjustment policies which are sometimes against their social development. In India, women constitute 70 per cent out of the people living below the poverty line. The persistence of extraordinarily high levels of gender inequality and female deprivation among India's most serious social failures. Hence, it is agreed that the empowerment of women is almost certainly the key. Women must have in their hands the right to make decisions. Therefore, it is highly imperative to evolve a strategy for providing a universal education for women, girls and labouring class people alongwith social security saftynets.

"Unorganised women labour in India" -- contains eleven papers, including one contribution of the editor. This volume examines the entire gamut of issues relating to women labourers, covering problems, development perspectives and policies.

Given the nature of topics discussed pertaining to the plight of unorganised women labourers and dimensional views displayed, the editor has retained from drawing any conclusion. This has been left to the readers.

The editor hereby expresses his sincere gratitude to the contributors for the pain that they have sustained in sparing their valuable time to put their ideas on "Women labourers down in the form of papers."

I shall feel rewarded, if the work is of some help in formulating policy measures for ameliorating the conditions of poor, downtrodden, exploited women labourers.

I express my thanks to Discovery Publishing House, New Delhi, for undertaking the work for publication. Lastly, I owe my indebtedness to Mr. H.K. Patro, Pinakin Commercial Type Institute, Berhampur, for taking the pain of neat typing.

S.N. TRIPATHY

1

Plight of Unorganized Women Workers

*Dr. I. Satya sundaram**

Indian women, constituting nearly half of the total population, play a vital role in the domestic sphere and also in the rural field, particularly in the agricultural sector. Yet, our traditional attitude is to treat women as second-class citizens. This is so in spite of the fact that women have proved their mettle in every walk of life. But, their contribution is not given due credit. According to an ILO estimate, the value of unpaid household work constitutes 25 to 39 per cent of GNP.

The largest number of working women in India is engaged in farming operations either as cultivators or as agricultural labourers. They take up a wide variety of activities like sowing of seeds, transplanting, weeding, harvesting, preparation of compost and manure pits, application of manures, storage of seeds and foodgrains. An active farm woman spends eight to mine hours on the farm during the peak agricultural season.[1]

I

Vital Role of Women Workers

Women's contribution to the economy by and large remains unrecognized. Yet, their services are valuable. Women account for over half the food produced in the developing world, and even more in Africa; they constitute one fourth of the developing world's industrial labour force; they carry the main responsibility for childcare and

* Research Director, Post-Graduate Department of Economics, The Hindu College, Machilipatnam, Andhra Pradesh.

household chores; they head one fourth or more of the families in many developing nations; and they usually fetch most of the household's water and fuelwood. Studies in Nepal and Philippines suggest that when the production of rural women is valued properly, on average, they actually contribute about one half of the family's income.[2]

The World Bank in its Annual Report in 1989 observed that 35 per cent of Indian houscholds below the poverty line are headed by women, and in most cases, are thus, dependent exclusively on female income. The Report observed that Women's contribution is significant in families having low economic status. The poorest families thus depend on women's economic productivity. The stress should therefore be on harnessing the strategic potential of women.

The World Bank Report further observed that making women more productive "will not merely reduce their dependency and enhance their status and security in the family, but also increase aggregate labour productivity in the family and accelerate growth in sectors, such as agriculture, where women constitute nearly half the labour force, increase household incomes, especially in families below the poverty line, increase the share of family income allocated to providing food and health care to children, improve male and female child survival and increase family investment in education for their daughters, and reduce fertility and slow population growth."

Some studies have shown that when women have access to income either through growing their own food crops or access to the wage in cash, the nutritional level of the family is much better than where women's access to home-grown food is replaced by cash income to the male head of household.[3]

The number of workers in the unorganized sector is increasing rapidly for various reasons. The firms and enterprises, in this highly competitive world, try to reduce costs. Certain aspects of the labour process are entrusted to cheap labour. The organized labour too is weak in the context of rising levels of open unemployment. Another factor contributing to the growth of informal sector is the rise of small enterprises like small retail shops, hotels and restaurants and repair shops. In these days of struggle for survival, the petty self-employment is also rapidly growing. Agriculture still employs women to the extent of 25 per cent of the unorganized work force, though growing mechanization has reduced the number of women workers in some operations.[4]

Nearly 92 per cent of the 317 million workers in the country belong to the unorganized sector. These workers therefore remain unprotected by law. They are the most vulnerable section of the society. These 290 million workers enjoy no job or income security with little bargaining power.

The unorganized workers include people involved in agriculture, and agriculture-related work, forest workers, fisherfolk, construction labourers, workers employed in small scale/ancillary units in the informal sector of industry, domestic workers, *anganwadi* workers, casual/contract labourers, home-based workers and self-employed workers.

According to the 1981 census, nearly 90 per cent of women work in the unorganized sector which does not offer fair wages and decent terms of work. Nor is there any opportunity to improve the earning potential. There is no supportive services like creches, fuel and water. In the sphere of farm family labour, women's contribution is immense, but no effort has been made to estimate this.

According to the 1991 census estimates, about 81 per cent of female workers are employed in agriculture as labourers or cultivators, constituting 87 per cent of the women workforce in rural areas and 17.5 per cent in urban areas.

The green revolution might have reduced women's work on the farm, but it has also enhanced the role of women in 'supportive activities'. In many places, the entire management of livestock are the work of women, unaided by men. This work is performed even during 'peak' seasons such as harvesting. Even in households where the new technology has raised incomes, no hired labour is used for these jobs. Women also perform all the post-harvest activities on the crops.[5]

Agriculture is becoming increasingly a female activity. Between 1971 and 1981, the ratio of female to male agricultural labour went up from 51 to 60 per cent. The ratio of female to male cultivators also rose from 14 to 19 per cent. By 1990, one out of three cultivators in Maharashtra was female. In Andhra Pradesh, Madhya Pradesh, Tamil Nadu and Karnataka, between 40 and 60 per cent of agricultural work is being done by women. In Maharashtra and Andhra Pradesh, female agricultural labour outnumbers male.[6]

II

Conditions of Women Workers

Many migrant domestic workers in cities live on pavements or in slums and serve others in houses. A woman domestic workers has to sweep, swab, wash utensils and clothes in every house twice a day - morning and evening. Sometimes, she has to stand in a long queue to get water. She has to repeat the same work in her own home and in other homes where she works. She has to put in extra work if guests stay on for several days. No extra remuneration for this. Women domestic workers often get a paltry sum for the unpleasant work they undertake. Some women domestic workers are sexually assaulted by their employers.[7]

A UN publication in 1980 has revealed the following facts about women all over the world. Women and girls are half the world's population, do two-thirds of the world's work hours, receive a tenth of the world's income and own less than a hundredth of the world's property. Two out of three of the world's illiterates were women.

In the developing world, women were responsible for 50 per cent of total food production. In Tanzania, women work an average of 2600 hours a year in agriculture, it is only 1800 hours a year for men. In Africa as a whole, 60 per cent of all agricultural work, 50 per cent of animal husbandry, and 100 per cent of food processing is done by women. For millions of women in the Third World - who cook and clean sew and wash, plant and weed, care for the old and bring up the young --- a 16 hour day is not uncommon.[8]

The unemployment rates among women are consistently higher than those among men. Statistics show that the status of women between three census (1971, 1981 and 1991) periods has marginally shifted from agriculture workers to unpaid family workers. The share of women in non-household industry improved during the three censual periods. The share of women in relatively better paying jobs in the transport, storage and communication sector shows a decline while its share in other services, after registering a decline, shows a marginal increase in the last census period. Thus women are sliding down to low paying or unpaid work.

The declining trend of women participation in the workforce may be due to the following three developments.[9]

(i) The technological and occupational structure of the economy might have undergone a male-biased transformation to such an extent that there has been a smaller expansion of the sectors where women workers have a relative advantage;

(ii) Indian economy has failed to attract many of potential women workers into the workforce. The growth in work participation is not in tune with growth in investment and output. This has naturally caused the composition of the labour force to be tilted in favour of the male; and

(iii) Urbanization is found to have dealt a severe blow to the rural household industries where women are normally found in large numbers. Also, there has been a declining trend in the sex ratio of the population.

TABLE - 1

Work Participation Rate in India

Year	*Category*	*Males*	*Females*
1971	Total	52.7	14.2
	Rural	53.8	15.9
	Urban	48.9	7.2
1981	Total	52.6	19.7
	Rural	53.8	23.1
	Urban	49.1	8.3
1991	Total	51.6	22.7
	Rural	52.5	27.2
	Urban	49.0	9.7

TABLE - 2

Unemployment Rates in India

Concept / Year	Rural Areas		Urban Areas	
	Males	*Females*	*Males*	*Females*
WEEKLY STATUS				
1961-62	3.7	8.5	3.0	3.3
1972-73	3.0	5.5	6.0	9.2
1977-78	3.6	4.0	7.1	10. 9
1983	3.7	4.3	6.7	7.5
1987-88	4.2	4.3	6.6	9.2

TABLE - 3

Percentage Distribution of Main Workers by Sectors

Sectors	*1971*		*1981*		*1991*	
	Males	*Females*	*Males*	*Females*	*Males*	*Females*
1	2	3	4	5	6	7
1. Cultivators	45.90	29.84	43.70	33.20	39.62	34.18
2. Agricultural Labourers	21.54	50.89	19.56	46.18	21.01	44.83
3. Livestock, Forestry & Fishing	2.24	1.91	2.34	1.85	1.94	1.58
4. Mining & Quarrying	0.54	0.40	0.62	0.35	0.69	0.31
5. Manufacturing						
A. Household Industry	3.42	4.24	3.18	4.59	2.08	3.49

(Contd.)

TABLE - 3 (contd.)

1	2	3	4	5	6	7
B. Non-household Industry	6.70	2.77	8.92	3.55	8.88	3.81
6. Construction	1.36	0.65	1.80	0.80	2.31	0.63
7. Trade & Commerce	6.37	1.78	7.33	2.04	8.93	2.22
8. Transport, Storage & Communication	2.84	0.47	3.32	0.38	3.51	0.31
9. Other Services	9.07	7.08	9.22	7.05	10.78	8.26
TOTAL	100.00	100.00	100.00	100.00	100.00	100.00

Source :
(i) Census of India, 1981
(ii) Census of India, 1991

TABLE - 4

All-India Workforce in Unorganised Sector in 1981 (in millions)

Sectors	*Male*	*Female*	*Total*
Agriculture	114.10 (75)	37.56 (25)	151.70 (100)
Manufacturing	16.80 (81)	4.30 (19)	21.10 (100)
Services	22.40 (84)	4.40 (16)	26.80 (100)
Total	153.30	46.26	199.56

Note : Figures in brackets are percentages to the total.

TABLE - 5

Female Employment by Status

Year	*Rural*			*Urban*		
	Self-employed	*Regular employees*	*Casual workers*	*Self-employed*	*Regular employees*	*Casual workers*
1972-73	64.5	4.1	31.4	48.5	27.8	23.7
1977-78	62.1	2.6	35.1	49.5	24.9	25.6
1983	61.9	2.8	35.3	45.8	25.8	28.4
1987-88	60.9	3.6	35.5	47.1	27.5	25.4

Source : Planning Commission Workers Paper, 'Employment Past Trends and Prospect for 1990s', New Delhi. May 1990. Table 7., p. 10

The status of women workers in India is clear from the fact that 94 per cent of them are engaged in the informal sector and only six per cent are in the organised sector. According to the census data, about 81 per cent female workers are employed in agriculture as cultivators or labourers, constituting 87 per cent of the women workforce in rural areas and 17.5 per cent in urban areas As compared to 1951, the percentage of women agricultural labourers has declined in 1991.

III
Women Workers : Major Problems

As per the census of 1981, only 14.44 per cent of women in the country are in gainful employment, a majority of whom remain confined to traditionally 'feminine' fields, which are often fields of low prestige, low economic returns and with poor scope for self development and upward mobility.

A general under-enumeration of women's involvement in gainful activity is due to confusion regarding the demarcation of 'domestic' from 'productive' work. In some countries, women work in agriculture, animal husbandry and marketing, water and fuel carrying, grain grinding etc. is completely ignored. Also, women's involvement in the cleaning and grading of agricultural produce contributes to the value added of articles sold in the market. Yet, such work is treated as 'domestic work'.[10]

Statistics relating to employment by status shows that between 1972 and 1988, the share of women in self-employment and in regular employment has declined. The share of women in casual employment has increased in rural and urban areas. Female employment in India is getting increasingly casualised. This phenomenon may be due to two reasons. First, the employers recruit women as casual workers in order to minimise the financial commitment. Second, with the increase in the sub-contracting of the production process, the employment in general, and that of women in particular, is being gradually transferred from the organised to the unorganised sector.[11]

Most unorganised workers work under adverse conditions. For instance, workers engaged in cleaning sewers may be killed by the noxious fumes that are often accumulated in the drains. This happens when the workers are not equipped with protective overalls or masks or when the mandatory test to ascertain the level of toxic gases in the drain are not conducted.[12]

The conditions of women workers worsened because of low literacy. According to the 1991 population census, female literacy rate was 39.42 as against 63.86 per cent for men. In absolute terms there were 197.3 million female illiterates while the number of male illiterates was 126.7 million. There has been further deterioration in the sex ratio (the number of females per thousand males) to 929 in 1991 from 934 in 1981. The disparity between male and female population has widened from nine million to 31 million during the period 1981 to 1991.

In some countries like South Africa, in the past, apartheid had adversely affected women's conditions. South African women were in the past the most overworked and under-paid section of the society. But, the African women did play a crucial role in the liberation struggle.[13]

The new agricultural technology has adversely affected women's participation in farm activities. The Committee on the Status of Women in India (1975) has observed, " ... another problem that affects women's participation in agriculture is the introduction of modern methods of cultivation, which is resulting in a gradual displacement of women and shrinking of their activities." Also, the new agricultural technology has not eliminated seasonality of work. On the other hand, it has only increased the extent of seasonal fluctuations in female employment.[14]

Till the 1980s, all over the world, on an average, women were found to earn about 60 per cent of the male wage for full-time work. The situation has not changed much over the years. Some believe that the wage differential is due to differences in human capital; others attribute it to differences in the social positions of men and women. This means that the difference is not market determined. [15] Even after adjustment for differences in hours of work, age and schooling, the earnings of women do not equal those of men. [16] The wage differential is there in respect of both agricultural and non-agricultural operations.[17]

It is a pity that women as wage earners in agricultural sector could not claim equal wages with their male counterparts. The reason given for this is that the output of woman is lower than that of men. But, studies show that in certain operations women are admittedly more efficient.[18]

However, it is observed that the average daily earnings of female child labour in agriculture were slightly higher than those of male child labour, probably because girls could do the better paid skilled tasks of women (e.g. transplanting) but boys could not do those of men (e.g. ploughing).[19]

IV

Measures Needed

The key to equality between men and women is the raising of the economic status of the latter. This is more true of the rural women.

The rural women can think of raising their socio-economic status only when they are educated. The programme for education of rural women should include information on: [20]

(i) specific agricultural practices;

(ii) economies in introducing new technology in agriculture and proper farm management;

(iii) nutritive values of food crops, animal products and fish and their importance in family diets;

(iv) basic principles of nutrition and how family diets can be improved by using local resources;

(v) raising of kitchen gardens for supply of nutritive vegetables throughout the year;

(vi) supplementing the income of family through subsidiary occupations like dairying, sheep, pig, goat keeping and poultry raising;

(vii) wastage in the family and its prevention;

(viii) child care and

(ix) relationship between a small family and socio-economic development.

More and more rural women need to be involved in self-employment. The self-employment in agriculture, village and small industries and retail trade and services should be expanded. Self-employment is also conducive to the development of individual initiative and entrepreneurial talent and offers greater personal freedom. Self-employment would enable women to combine their dual role of producer and home maker without stress. The majority of self-employment women will engage in home based productive activity. Also, home-based self-employment for women, by avoiding increasing interaction between the sexes, would not disturb the institution of family.[21]

The World Bank made certain recommendations, in its Annual Report in 1989, to improve the productive capacity of women in India. These include :

- provision of direct access to institutional credit;
- orientational and operational modifications in the agricultural research and agricultural extension systems;
- the promotion of direct membership in viable producer cooperatives; and
- organization of women into groups that provide them a legitimate forum beyond the private domestic sphere and a more audible voice in demanding services and inputs.

In the rural context, organization of the poor assumes special significance as the unorganised labourers are the victims of poverty and unemployment. It has been rightly observed, "Organization of the rural poor is required to secure their full participation in the execution of government plans for integrated rural development. This is by itself deemed capable to solve the problem of unemployment and poverty. It also would guarantee the effective functioning of an alternative delivery system to help the poor population directly."[22]

There is also need for strengthening grassroots initiatives as they provide a potential for change even though their wide impact remains to be seen.[23]

More productive employment on a durable basic appears to be the only panacea to the pitiable plight of the unorganised. Women workers who can seek better treatment only through collective action. The opportunities for wage employment are limited. Hence, problems of women workers in the self-employment sector deserve immediate attention.

References

1. Shanti Chakravarty : 'Women Power in Agriculture', Kurukshetra, November 16, 1975. p. 8.

2. Barbara Herz : 'Bringing Women into the Economic Mainstream', *Finance & Development*, December 1989. p. 22.

3. Leela Phadnis and Faculty, Home Science College, University of Agricultural Sciences, Dharwar, Karnataka. 1977.

4. Sudha Kumari : 'Women Workers in Unorganised Sector in India', *Yojana*, July 1-15, 1989. p. 11.

5. Sudha Pai : 'Women on Small Family Farms', *Mainstream*, December, 9, 1989. p. 30.

6. Shahnaz Anklesaria Aiyar : 'Agenda of Priorities for Women', Indian Express, January 7, 1990.

7. Jean D' Cunha : "Domestic Workers : Isolated and Powerless", *Indian Express* (Magazine Section), July 5, 1987.

8. Kurukshetra, July 16, 1980.

9. Satyabrata Rai Chowdhuri : 'Women's Place in the Labour Market', *Indian Express*, May 13, 1995.

10. Bina Agarwal : 'Work Participation of Rural Women in Third World : Some Data and Conceptual Biases', *Economic and Political Weekly*, December 21-28, 1985. p.-157.

11. Gopal Singh, Shyam P. Sharma and Prem R. Bhardwaj : 'Structural Adjustment and Female Workers', *Mainstream*, February 19, 1994. p. 30.

12. Ammu Joseph : 'A Voice for the Unheard', *The Hindu* (Magazine Section) August 20, 1995.

13. Sheela Reddy : 'Apartheid and Women: The Third Dimension', *Mainstream*, April 13, 1985. p. 32.

14. Nata Duvvury : 'Women in Agriculture: A Review of the Indian Literature', *Economic and Political Weekly*, October 28, 1989. p. WS-102.

15. Aneesha : 'Why Do Women Get Jobs ?', *The Economic Times* (Mid Week Review), April 7, 1988.

16. Sudha Kumari : op. cit. p.12.

17. Narayan Prasad Sharma : 'Wage Differentials for Women Agricultural Labourers', *Yojana*, July 1-15, 1989. p. 9.

18. Shanti Chakravarty : op. cit. p. 8.

19. *Sarvekashana*, 1981, p. 5126.

20. Shanti Chakravarty : op. cit. p. 12.

21. Pushpa Sundar : 'Women's Employment and Organization Modes', *Economic and Political Weekly*, November 26,1983.p.m. - 171.

22. Volken : 'Mass Poverty in Rural India : Organization of the Rural Poor in the Context of the Existing Power Structure', Social Action, January-March 1983. p.11.

23. Bina Agarwal : 'Rural Women, Poverty and Natural Resources : Sustenance, Sustainability and Struggle for Change', *Economic and Political Weekly*, October 28, 1989. p. WS-60.

2

Unorganised Women Workers : Problems and Prospects

Dr. Nancy David *

Institutional theories relating to female labour market developed by Piore and Doeringer state that labour market consists of two main sectors which has been labelled as primary and secondary. The primary sector consists of large firms all displaying a degree of market power. Employees in this sector enjoy relatively high quality working conditions; including high wage, stable employment, established promotion opportunities and participation in establishing the administrative rules governing their work environment.

The Secondary sector generally consists of small peripheral firms that typically perform lowly skilled work task and are constantly threatened by potential competitors. Workers in these firms face unattractive work packages with low wages unstable employment, little chance of promotion and arbitrary managerial decision making. The unsatisfactory working pattern of secondary sector limits the chances of employees being employed in the primary market.

This dual labour market theoretical approach can very well be applied to the organised and unorganised sector of the developing economies. The unorganised sector also called the *informal sector, traditional sector and unregulated sector*. It is not easy to provide a strict definition of unorganised sector. According to an ILO study (1972) as published in Meier (1984) the characteristics of unorganised sector are "ease of entry, reliance on indigenous resources, family ownership of

* Professor of Economics, Mother Teresa Women University, Kodaikanal.

enterprises small scale operations, labour intensive and adapted technology, skills acquired outside the formal school system and regulated and competitive markets."

Historically, the economic development of western Europe and North America has often been described interms of the continuous transfer of economic activity and people from rural to urban areas. As urban industries expanded, new employment opportunities were created while labour saving technological progress in agriculture reduced rural man-power needs. The combination of these two phenomena made it possible for western nations to undergo an orderly and effective rural to urban transfer of their human resources leading to the emergence of a modern industrial sector. Unfortunately this strategy of industrialization has in most instances of developing nations failed to bring about the desired results. More significantly regulatory labour polices that have slowed employment growth in the industrial sector. In countries like India the industrial sector fail to absorb the surplus or displaced agricultural labourer because of its limited capacity to generate employment. These labourers mostly unskilled find their survival in the unorganised sector. This is very true in the case of women workers. Growth in female agricultural employment has out paced female job creation in the rest of the economy. Among the reasons are the absolescence of many non-agricultural occupations dominated by women and the movements of men in to new mechanized jobs that have replaced these jobs. Women's lack of education and training as well as stereotypes about their ability to master mechanical and technical skills (Anker 1985) have been major barrier to upward mobility.

There are varied views on the emergence and role of the informal sector in the developing countries. The liberalization strategies and the control in the formal sector make the informal sector to grow. The emergence of informal economics cannot be explained without reference to formal policies of Governments. To the extent that the aspriations of the people are thwarted by the polices of the Governments, the population of participants in informal economics will grow (Jenkins, 1985).

The Structure and Composition of the Unorganised Sector

The difference between organised and unorganised sector is

based on the organization and nature of problems in employment in this sector. The difference between these two is not functional as between agriculture industry and services because these functions may be found in both the sectors. According to the Committee on the Status of Women 1974, "the real difference between them lies in the organization of productive relations, the degree of penetration of public control and regulations and recognition of data collective agencies and scientific investigation."

Labouring women in the informal sector are an important segment on the labour force. According to an estimate of the National Commission on Self Employment of Women, 94 per cent of the total female work force operates in the unorganised sector. They do arduous work as wage earners, piece rate workers, casual labour and paid family labour. The coverage of labour laws has not benefited these women workers in many areas of wages, working conditions, maternity benefits and social security.

According to the National Commission on Self Employed Women the unprotected workers include all those who are outside the preview of the organised sector. By the nature of their activities, they can be classified under the following broad categories (a) home based producers including artisans and piece-rate workers, entrepreneurs of Micro enterprises paid and unpaid family labourers (b) petty vendors and hawkers (c) contract labour and casual labour (d) domestic helpers, scavengers, washerwomen (e) those doing manual work like construction labour and those working in agriculture and other primary sectors (f) women engaged in processing work in traditional and non-traditional areas. On the basis of the employment status the aforesaid group can be classified under three catagories : (a) the self-employed (b) wage earners working outside their home and working inside the home perhaps in the form of micro enterprises and (c) unpaid family helpers. The unorganised sector presents two problems to policy makers. First an increasingly large segment of the working population is being forced to live at the margin of survival. Second given the availability of such cheap labour in the unorganised sector, employees are likely to divert more activities to such organizations. This would mean that the working class as a whole will in future receive an ever declining share in the products of development. No popular Government can afford to ignore these possibilities for long (Nirmala Bannerjee, 1985)

Sometimes the unorganised sector is divided into institutionalised unorganised sector and non-institutionalised unorganised sector. The components of institutionalised unorganised sectors are agriculture, agriculture based industries, construction work, small industrial units like beedimaking, domestic matches, tailoring garment units, food processing units and other registered units. These units are supposed to implement measures like minimum wages and regulation on working hours but not effectively enforcing them. The non-institutionalised unorganised sector comprises workers doing casual work like the domestic workers, sweepers, scavengers, vendors, and hawkers and those who are self-employed.

The concentration of women workers on the informal sector occupations is not due to their choice but because there is no other alternative for them and they are working all through their lives in such jobs. Studies on unorganised sector high light the fact that usually the urban segments of the unorganised sector and rural sector are treated very often separately. Or many studies deal with rural women and urban women and their working condition. Agriculture and allied activities also fall in the category of unorganised labour market activities and it is necessary to mention about the female agricultural worker while discussing about the nature and significane of unorganised sector. Female agricultural labourers are indeed among the poorest section of Indian society with the lowest wage levels (about three fourth of the male rate) and highest unemployment. Poverty is pushing a growing number of women into agricultural wage workers who were not previously in the labour force or were self-employed as cultivator or artisans. This trend is often referred as the feminization of the agricultural labour force. Despite their increasing prominence in the agricultural labour force rural women are not being absorbed in many of the jobs outside agriculture that are developing in the rural areas. These avenues of employment often require specific skills that women do not have. Women also have not been socialised to seek out and adopt to non-traditional work situtions. Agricultural female labour under such conditions often migrate and incorporate themselves at the margin of the urban economy. The major avenue of employment for these women lies in the urban informal sector. Even for the informal sector employment competition is intense and most of the women are employed in activities that take very specific forms. They tend to concentrate in areas of non-wage sector that are compatiable with their reproductive role particularly child rearing and often extension of their domestic responsibilities within the household.

There is an age specific female work force in the unorganised market. There has been an over whelming concentration of young women in the world market factories, that is factories which export to the international market. This kind of employment for many women has brought about a break with the past an opportunity for earning cash income and greater independence. However, in terms of working condition, many of the intricate mechanisms of gender-based subordination continue to operate.

Studies that have been done on the sexual division of labour in a number of informal sector activities found that the kind of non-wage labour in which low income women are concentrated are those which have involved skills developed within the households. Men's economic activity in the informal sector requires a higher capital investment than women's. Women are mainly found in the domestic services, sellling of furits and vegetables, in the selling of cooked food and petty trading as well as in the textile and tailoring sector. Most of this work can be carried out by women in their own homes and be part of family consumption.

Women in out work forms another very large percentage in the informal sector. Out work involves putting out all or part of the production process from a central point to several small units. This process is part of the strategy to cut labour costs to overcome problems of capital investment and to survive in competitive market. By putting out its work big industrial units take advantage not only of low wages, in security of employment and lack of social benefits but also a long working hours. Out workers in Asia are predominantly women and children.

Unorganised sector comprises nearby two thirds of self-employed women. The rapid increase in unemployment has recently led to emphasis on the need to promote self-employment and Government is providing assistance through training and credit facilities. Self-employment is successful only where women are in a position to market their products. The efforts of welfare organisation in this regard deserve appreciation. Of late, it is said that the micro enterprise sector has emerged within the unorganised sector and it creates substantial wage employment. Inspite of Governments effort to promote micro enterprises owned by women entrepreneurs in the informal sector they are invariably inhibited by a number of constraints related essentially with infrastructure, marketing, availability of basic inputs and finance.

The project on 'Integrated Strategies of Employment Generation and Poverty Alleviation in India' sponsored by the UNDP and implemented by ILO-ARTEP has assessed the manifestation of informal characteristics in the urban economy and analysed the specific sectors that are to have a large incidence of unorganised employment. The trend towards informalisation has been assessed in terms of growth of casual and self employed workers, of weekly status workers and of female and child workers induced largly by poverty. Studies based on secondary data suggest that unorganised sector has grown at faster rate than the organised sector in the Indian economy. The study by the planning commission 1990 reveals that the annual growth of employment in the unorganised sector was 2.21 per cent compared to 2.11 per cent in the organised sector during 1971-77 were very high viz 2.84 per cent and 2.48 per cent. The rates were however much lower during 1983-87. Nonetheless, the percentage growth in the unorganised sector was 1.55 higher than that of the organised sector which was 1.36 only. The urban employment has grown at a faster rate than the rural areas, largely due to the growth of the unorganised sector.

The most significant trend in the urban labour market is increasing casualisation of male work force. The changes in the nature of employment of urban female are quiet different. Here the percentage of casual workers among all (usual status) workers has gone down in non-agricultural activities over the years. The share of regular employment outside agriculture has increased while in agriculture it has gone down.

The growth in employment has taken place largely in low productive sector having a high incidence of informal employment.

Percentage Distribution of Usually Employed Persons as per Principal and Subsidiary Status Across Employment Categories in Di.:ferent NSS Rounds.

Employment Categories	Male					Female				
	1972-1973	*1977-1978*	*1983*	*1987-1988*	*1989-1990*	*1972-1973*	*1977-1978*	*1983*	*1987-1988*	*1989-1990*
Self Employed	39.2	40.4	40.9	41.6	42.3	48.4	49.5	45.8	47.1	48.6
(a) Agriculture	6.4	6.4	6.2	5.5	6.2	-	18.7	15.4	16.1	13.6
	-	(58.6)	(62.9)	(63.4)	(62.0)	-	(58.6)	(56.0)	(60.8)	(56.3)
(b) Non-Agriculture	-	34.0	34.7	36.1	36.1	-	30.8	30.4	30.1	35.0
	-	(37.8)	(38.4)	(39.6)	(40.1)	-	(45.2)	(41.9)	(42.4)	(46.1)
Regular /Salaried	*50.7*	*46.4*	*43.7*	*43.7*	*41.3*	*27.9*	*24.9*	*25.8*	*27.5*	*28.9*
(a) Agriculture	-	1.0	0.6	0.6	0.5	-	0.8	0.5	0.3	0.3
		(10.0)	(9.4)	(6.1)	(5.2)	-	(2.5)	(1.8)	(1.2)	(1.5)
(b) Non -Agriculture	-	45.4	43.1	43.1	40.8	-	24.1	25.3	27.1	28.6
		(51.4)	(48.2)	(47.2)	(45.3)		(35.5)	(34.8)	(37.2)	(37.6)
Casual workers	*10.1*	*13.2*	*15.4*	*14.6*	*16.5*	*23.7*	*25.6*	*28.4*	*25.4*	*22.5*
(a) Agriculture	-	3.2	2.9	2.6	3.3		12.4	11.6	10.1	10.2
		(31.4)	(27.8)	(30.5)	(32.7)	-	(39.0)	(42.2)	(37.9)	(42.2)
(b)Non-Agriculture	-	10.0	12.4	12.0	13.2	-	13.1	16.8	15.3	12.3
		(10.8	(13.4)	(13.2)	(14.7)		(19.3)	(23.2)	(20.4)	(16.2)

Notes : The figur are computed using the data from *Sarvekshana*, September 1950 and Visaria and Minhas (1991)
Figures in the brackets are percentage to the total workers in agriculture and non-agriculture.

Problems of Women Workers in the Unorganised Sector

The concentration of women in informal sector occupations that are characterised by low wages, low capital intensiveness low energy and use of crude technology. Home based production employing women workers lacks visibility depends mostly on merchant contractors or industrial capitalist, and subject to non-applicability of labour legislation, loss of employment and involvement of family labour often turn out to be unpaid labour.

Self-employed workers unlike some of the home based workers and the workers in the casual wage sector do not have an indentifiable employer-employees relationship. The relationship available appears to be with the state and the oppression of power group is inevitable.

Wage employment includes women working in construction and domestic service and women employed in rural areas as agricultural casual labourer. Such employment are not employment but 'Coolie work' and these workers are no wonder remain marginalised both in the impact of development efforts as well as mobilisation activities of the more organised trade unions.

Women working in the unorganised sector lack supportive service like creches and child care centres where women could leave their children during working hours. Sexual harassment is very acute in the sector. Contractors exploit young girls even women, and women many a situation circumvent to their lust. Lack of organisation also hampers the bargaining power and the power to resist exploitation. Banerjee observes that social neglect of these women as workers is evident from the fact that a large percentage has never found any organisation interested in them as workers nor had they ever heard the possible benefits of such activities from leader who could inspire their confidence. Mobilisation strategies based on the logic of 'struggle through development are not of the view that the existing structural context provides for mobilisation through the use of certain existing instruments. These also strengthen the economic base and to some extent diminish the vulnerability of women. This strategy does not directly confront the elements of power but attempts to strengthen the powerless by bringing them to a state preparedness. (Kalpayam 1994).

SEWA in Ahmadabad and working Women's Forum (WWF) in Madras and few other Non-Governmental Organisations are worth mentioning in this regard. Wage discrimination is also widely prevalent in the unorganised sector and it is more pronounced in agricultural operations. Discrimination in wages is said to exist when men and women are paid differently for doing the same job. Normally women are paid low wages in agriculture on account of cheap labour and also the traditional classifications of certain jobs as the monopoly of women. The following table shows wage differential in the average wage earnings per day in 1983 (in rupees) between male and female workers.

Category	*Rural*		*Urban*	
	Male	*Female*	*Male*	*Female*
Regular wage Employees	15.04	10.11	28.30	16.86
Casual wage Labour	10.27	4.89	11.09	5.29

Source : National Sample Survey Organisation 1987.

Policy Implications

Jobs in the rapidly growing informal sector provide work and income for the majority of urban women workers. Conservative estimates based on 1981 census, suggest that 53 per cent of the female urban labour force in the informal sector : NSS data for 1983 shows the proportion to be high as 75 per cent. Poor women are especially dependent on informal sector employment. Social indepth studies conducted in different cities showed that about 70 per cent of the women working in informal sector occupations were below the poverty line (Bapat and Crook 1988).

Although there are important variations between different subsectors with regard to literacy, health problems, education levels and remunerations, Their variations occurs within a narrow interval with averages that clearly indicate the disadvantaged positions of these women. Their earnings and job security are low, hours long, life time earning profiles, flat and working conditions, physically stressful and often unhealthy Government awareness of this situation has grown with the recent publication of the Report of the National Commission on self-employed women and women in the Informal Sector (GOI, 1988)

The official response has so far generally centered on proposals to extend the regulatory protection covering formal sector workers to encompass these disadvantaged women. Women's activist groups many of whom contributed to the commission's work have also supported this view. Extending regulating protection to informal sector workers has unfortunately, not, proved to be effective in the past. The minimum wage legislative in one salient example. World Bank (1989) argues the controls imposed on manufacturing units compel them to use casual labour rather than permanent employees wherever possible and to engage in dispersed production through small unregulated firms and home based workers. Even if it were possible to enforce labour regulations throughout the informal sector, in a labour market crowded with unskilled workers, that low-wages work force will continue to exist. The formal and informal duality will remain in all possibility women will continue to be concentrated in the informal sector.

It is suggested that the industrial sector to adopt more labour intensive production methods and create more jobs than defensive job saving approach. Among the specific measures proposed is the gradual dismantling of all but a few basic and enforceable regulations to protect workers and applying these too all workers, thereby gradually weakening the formal informal duality.

The critical question is whether this approach would improve the jobs, wages and quality of life for poor women. Overall growth in the economy is undoubtedly a necessary condition for any lasting improvement in the employment and income situation of poor women working in the informal sector. But, as the CEM recognize it will not be sufficient by itself to reduce gender-based disparities and distribute more equitably the benefits of growth. Given women's disadvantage in terms of education, skills, and mobility, as well as the restrictive social attitudes they confront, it is unlikely that they will get the new jobs that the suggested reforms would open up in the formal sector.

To ensure that accelerated industrial growth such as India has experienced over the past decade (yearly rate of over 8 per cent in the 1980s) directly benefits the poor, the CEM recommended a set of policies to reduce the bias against labour-intensive rather than capital-intensive investment. Especially important for women, who are concentrated in the informal sector, is the removal of regulatory barriers that discourage ancillary relationships between small and large firms and inhabit expansion of successful firms in the informal and small-scale sectors. Policies such as product reservation and subsidized credit that are meant to assist the small-scale sector in the belief that it is highly labour intensive and will create employment for the poor are shown to act instead as incentives for small-scale firms to remain small and invest in capital intensive production.

In addition to changes in the macro-level industrial policy environment to promote employment growth, there may be a need for measures to ensure that gender-specific constraints to female employment are addressed. As an extension of efforts to increase the employment potential of firms of all sizes, it will also be important to enable poor women (and men) to create their own jobs-through providing better access to education, credit, land, extension advice, technology, raw materials, and markets. If women obtain this access, they can and will create their own jobs and make these jobs more productive and therefore more remunerative.

India must develop an integrated view of the manufacturing and service sectors. It must emphasize the ways in which policies enacted to regulate or benefit one segment, affect the potential for growth, and job creation in another. Policy changes are imperative to improve both wage and self-employment in the formal and informal sector. Given the remarkable vitality of the informal sector, there is a need for more precise understanding of it and of its complex relationship with the formal sector.

If women are to claim a larger share of new jobs generated over the long term, especially in the formal sector and in nontraditional occupations, the disparities in male and female access to education and technical training must be addressed immediately on a massive scale. Measures are also needed to address other gender-specific constraints to women's employment. Most of these measures fall into the same broad categories as those proposed to support rural women. They include access to institutional finance and skill training, supportive services such as day-care for children, quality health and family planning service, group formation, and advocacy to bring the needs and achievements of women to the attention of policymakers. In addition, urban women often face legal barriers regarding the hours and conditions of their employment that need to be removed.

References

1. Michel Piore : Labour Market Segmentation to what Paradigm does it belong ? American Economic Review 73, 1983. p.249.

2. Doeringer : Determinants of the Structure of Industrial Type Labour Markets. Industrial and Labour Relations Review 20, 1967. p. 206.

3. Meier, Gerald M (1984) Leading Issues in Economic Development. Oxford University Press.

4. Jenkin Jerry (1985) Women in the third world, Paths to a better future. Paper for USAID.

5. Nirmal Banerjee (1985) Women in the Unorganised Sector. Delhi, Sangam Books.

6. Project Report on Integrated Strategies of Employment Generation and Poverty Alleviation in India.

7. Kalpagam. U., Labour and Gender Survival in Urban India. Sage Publication 1994.

8. Bapat, Meera and Nigel Crook (1988). The Quality of Female Employment Evidence from a Study in Pune EPW Vol. 23 No. 31. p. 1595.

9. GOI (Govt. of India) (1974) Towards equality - New Delhi.

10. CEM (1989) Country Economic Memorandum.

11. World Bank (1989) India Poverty Employment and Social Service Report 7617 Washington DC.

12. Lynn Bennett : Women poverty and productivity In India EDC Seminar Paper No. 43. World Bank. 1994.

3

Rural Women and Development

Dr. Hemalatha Prasad *

Introduction

Women are vital and productive workers in India's economy. They make up one-third of the labour force. The Five Year Plans have consistently placed special emphasis on providing minimum health facilities, integrated with family welfare, nutrition and education for women and children. Various welfare and development services have been introduced to improve living conditions of women and to increase their access to and control over material and social resources. Special steps have been taken to remove legal, social and other constraints to enable them to make use of the rights and new opportunities becoming available for them.

Various studies show that women are becoming increasingly conscious of their rights and capabilities. However, the demographic features of female population like excessive mortality in female children resulting in persistent decline in sex ratio, low rate of literacy. Therefore, low economic status of women cannot be raised without opening up of opportunities of independent employment and income for them. But the process of change to raise the status of women under various spheres of socio-economic activities would require sustained efforts and political will over a period of time.

* Faculty of Women's Studies, National Institute of Rural Development, Hyderabad.

Historical Background

In the wake of independence from colonial rule in 1947, the leaders of the nation set about harmonising the need for modernisation and development with peoples needs. While industrial growth and investment in infrastructure were the foundations of national efforts. Post independence decade, this periods was also marked by the establishment of the Central Social Welfare Board in 1953 to spearhead welfare measures for women. In keeping with the welfare approach to women's problems, the CSWB as a grant in aid body was to provide assistance to voluntary agencies and welfare societies to establish services and infrastructure for the welfare of women. The adoption of community development measures also heralded the organisation of women into Mahila Mandals, irrespective of class or caste distinctions.

The Second Five Year Plan[3] (1956-1961) was closely linked with the overall approach of intensive agricultural development. The plan recognised the need for the organisation of women as workers. It also perceived the social prejudices/disabilities they suffered. The plan stated that women should be protected against injurious work, should receive maternity benefits and creches for children. It also suggested speedy implementation of the principle of equal pay for equal work and provision for training to enable women to compete for higher jobs.

The Third and the Fourth Five Year Plans accorded a high priority to education of women. Measures to improve maternal and child health services, supplementary feeding for children and nursing and expectant mothers were introduced. The Fifth Plan supported economic development, employment and training for women as the principal focus for their socio-economic development. The main approach in these plans was generally to view women as the beneficiaries of social services rather than as contributors to development.

Through the mid 1970s, there was no major change in the programmes for rural women. The year 1975 may be considered a watershed in the development of government policies and programmes for women in India. In late 1974, the committee on the status of women in India (CSWI) submitted its report *Towards Equality*, in the context of observance of the International Women's year in 1975 and the preparation of a National Plan of Action for Women. The creation of a separate Bureau of Women's Development and the setting up of a national committee with the Prime Minister as President were intended to provide strong administrative support to women's development.

During the Sixth plan (1980-85) multi-sectoral approach was adopted for women's development and separate Department of Women's Welfare was carved out of the centre in 1985 from the then existing Ministry of Social and Women's Welfare to give a separate identity and to provide a nodal point on matters relating to women's development. Legislative measures were taken to provide protection to women against discrimination, exploitation, atrocities and violence. Various legislations were amended to safeguard the interests of women and provide for their welfare.

A strategy of direct attack on poverty was adopted in the Sixth Plan as the theory of trickle down benefits of general development programmes had not proved as a successful strategy for the removal of poverty. Forty eight per cent of the population were found to be living below the poverty line. Women's employment has been recognised as the critical entry point for women's integration in mainstream development. The low and deteriorating status of rural women is attributed to their declining economic participation and other factors like the modernization of the agricultural sector. It is now accepted that the participation of women themselves in the development activities is the most effective tool for the promotion of the access of women to the benefits of development.

The IRDP initiated in 1978-79 and extended to all the developmental blocks in the country in 1980-81 was conceived as one of the instruments for the direct attack on poverty under IRDP, a special place was given for training rural unemployment youth for Employment with the introduction of TRYSEM. An exclusive scheme for the social and economic uplift of women belonging to families below the poverty line, Development of Women and Children in Rural Areas (DWCRA) was launched in 1982 as a sub-component of IRDP.

The Seventh Plan (1986-1991) continued this strategy. The National Perspective Plans for Women (1988-2000) provides directions for all round development of women. The National Commission on Self-Employed Women and Women in Informal Sector submitted a comprehensive report titled "Shramshakti", analysing the problems affecting large number of women in the informal sector and the steps needed to give them a better deal. A significant step taken in the seventh Plan towards improving women's status was the identification of a number of beneficiary obtained programmes under various sectors of development.

Entrepreneurship Development Programme

One of the measures to improve employment and earnings of women, a separate entrepreneurs' cell has been set up in the office of the Development Commission, Small Scale Industries to provide counselling to women entrepreneurs. Development of Entrepreneurship among women is also been encouraged by Small Industries Department organisation by organising entrepreneurs development programmes exclusively for women. Women are given preference in schemes of self-employment among educated unemployed youth introduced in 1983-84.

Support to Training and Employment Programme (STEP)

An ambitious scheme Support to Training and Employment Programme (STEP) was initiated for rendering support to women's employment in sectors such as agriculture, dairying, small animal husbandry, fisheries, kadhi and village industries, handlooms, handicrafts and sericulture. It focuses on the poorest and most marginalised women.

Women Development Corporations

Women Development Corporations were established with an objective of making women economically independent and self-reliant. The corporations identify women entrepreneurs and viable projects, facilitate availability of credit, promote marketing, and arrange training in trades, project formulation, management, etc.

Welfare Services

For improving the health and nutrition status of women, maternal and child health services were strengthened. Under the scheme of prophylaxis against nutritional anaemia, pregnant and nursing mothers were given a daily dose of iron and folic acid for 100 days. Camps were organised for women to create health awareness among them. The universal immunization programme, which aims at universal coverage of pregnant women and infants was extended to all districts in the country.

A number of schemes, supplementing to the general development programmes were implemented by the Department of Women and Child Development. The Accelerated Rural Water Supply Programme (ARWSP) and the Minimum Needs Programme (MNP) are of special significance to rural women who are the victims of drudgery, such as fetching water from distant locations. The Technology Mission on Drinking water and Related water management lays emphasis on purification of water to make it potable, training in the use of water and maintenance of water sources. The low cost sanitation programme is also of great importance to women, who are otherwise subjected to a lot of privacies due to lack of appropriate sanitation facilities.

Present Developments

Eighth plan strategy involved a deliberate attempt to ensure that benefits from different sectors did not bypass women. Special plans are being implemented to complement general development programmes which themselves have been constituted to be gender-sensitive. The flow of benefits to women in education, health and employment are being closely monitored. Women must be enabled to function as equal partners to men and should be treated as participants in development rather than as beneficiaries of schemes. Another important objective of eighth plan was to extend the reach of services to women qualitatively and quantitatively. Voluntary agencies are being supported in their advocacy and social activism programmes for gender equality and prevention of atrocities on women.

A separate Department of Women and Child Development within the Ministry of HRD has nodal responsibility of coordinating programmes for development and welfare of women as well as activities of different Ministries / Departments at the Centre and in States to promote appropriate programmes for women's development. The thrust is in provision of the following services aimed at women's development.

(i) Employment and income generating projects.
(ii) Education and training.
(iii) Support services ;
(iv) Awareness generation ;
(v) Legal aid.

The Department also monitors 27 beneficiary oriented schemes for women identified by the Prime Minister's Office such as :

Rural Development

1. Development of Women and Children in Rural Areas (DWCRA).

Education

2. Non-formal education exclusively for girls.

Family Welfare

3. Training of Auxiliary Nurse Midwives (ANM's), midwives, and Lady Health Visitors (LHV's).
4. Training of dais.
5. Immunization with TT for expectant mothers.
6. Village Health Guide Scheme.

Labour and Labour Welfare Sector

7. Vocational Training for Women.
8. Diversification and Extension of the Vocational Training Programmes for Women (including RVTI's).
9. Establishment of RVTI at Hissar (Haryana).
10. Establishment of placement cells and conducting training needs assessment surveys at NVT's / RVTI's.
11. Establishment of additional RVTI's.
12. Strengthening of RVTI for women at New Delhi and RVTI's at Bombay and Bangalore.
13. Grants-in-aid to State Governments for establishing women ITI's.

Employment Services

14. Rehabilitation of Handicapped women (selling up 2 VRCs for women).

Development of Backward classes

15. Girl's hostels.

Deptt. of Women and Child Development

16. Hostels for working women.
17. Employment and income generation training-cum-production centres.
18. Condensed courses of education.
19. Socio-economic programmes.
20. Awareness generation for Rural and poor women.
21. Women's Development Corporation.
22. Rehabilitation of women in distress.
23. Short stay homes.
24. Creches.

Science and Technology

25. Application of science and technology for women.
26. Backyard Poultry Development.

Social Forestry

27. Tree pattas.

Policy and Programme Initiatives (1994-95)

1. *Mahila Samruddhi Yojana (MSY)* : To enable rural women to have control over their savings and financial resources, the MSY offers facilities of small deposits, at attractive rate of interest (25 per cent), through the extensive network of rural post offices. An incentive of Rupees 75 is provided for an amount of Rupees 300 deposited for a continuous period of 12 months. During 1994-95, it is proposed to get 12 lakh accounts opened by women with deposit mobilisation of Rupees 12 crores.

2. *Rashtriya Mahila Kosh (RMK)* : Under the RMK, credit is extended to poor women at reasonable rates of interest through voluntary organisations working in rural areas. During 1994-95, 25 volun-

tary organisations will receive loans to assist 5000 poor women both in rural and urban areas at an interest rate of 12%.

3. *National creche Fund* : Government of India have established the Fund for establishment of creches in work places and rural areas through voluntary organisations. The programme also aims at converting Anganwadis into Anganwadi-cum-Creches. During 1994-95, it is proposed to open 500 in existing Anganwadis in the Government sector with an outlay of Rupees 130 lakhs.

4. *National Children Fund (NCF)* : It is proposed to submit proposals under NFC for grant of Rupees 1 lakh per agency to 10 voluntary agencies during 1994-95 to take up activities in the area of child welfare such as health care, education, recreation facilities etc.

Poverty and Economic Deprivation

Women perform triple roles that comprise of :

(i) biological reproduction
(ii) cyclical and repetitive household chores ; and
(iii) community networking for survival.

Against this backdrop of multiple roles, the inequalities appear profound. The inequalities that women suffer in the demographic reproduction system is also witnessed in equal intensity in the material reproduction system, where the two inequalities reinforce each other. The intensity in the material production system manifests itself not only in the unequal wage rates but lack of, or inadequate access to, government subsidies, subsidised credit, technologies that can enhance their productivity levels and investments in areas that can reduce drudgery and help increase time for productive work which can increase incomes, enable better supervision and care of children or rest. The cycle of poverty affects mostly such women of poor households living in backward areas. Poverty not only induces malnutrition but also forces women to work as well as bear the burden of household work involves collection of fuel and water, requiring very often long distances of walking, since the backward areas are also normally environmentally the most depleted. In such economies, the opportunity cost of the time spent on household work is high. Programmes that arrest the increasing denudation of trees and soils, restore environmental balance and reduce levels of absolute poverty have a direct bearing on achieving a better living standard for women.

Poverty Alleviation Programmes and Self-Employment

Poverty alleviation programmes were designed to directly benefit those below poverty line as development benefits were not accruing to the rural poor. The main stream poverty programmes can be categorised into those specially designed for women such as DWCRA ; those with specific targets for women such as IRDP and TRYSEM and finally programmes which do not have any specific numerical targets and open to women, such as JRY.

Development of Women and Children in Rural Areas (DWCRA)

It was in recognition of the fact that rural development programmes were not reaching the poorest women that the Development of Women and Children in Rural areas was launched as a sub-component of IRDP. DWCRA was started as pilot scheme in 50 selected districts in all states in 1982-83 and was extended in phased manner.

The objective of the programme is to organise women socio-economic activity groups with the dual objective of the providing self-employment opportunities and social strength to them (Seventh Plan Document). DWCRA's aim therefore, to organise women into groups for the effective utilization of credit under IRDP. Besides providing financial support for income generating, it also aims to increase women's to other government programs and welfare services. The program envisages formation of a group of 10-15 women. While the common interest that brings the group together may or may not be income generation, the support provided by DWCRA is intended to enhance the income generating capability of women in the group. The asst. project officer, Mukhya sevikas and gram sevikas are expected to spend adequate time in educating the women and to give special attention to the problems of the women's group and discuss proposed solutions. Each group is expected to identify a group organiser, who will take the responsibility of liaison work.

A grant of Rs. 15,000 is given to each group for a revolving fund to be used for purchase of raw material, marketing, child care etc.

The amount is shared equally by Central grant, state grant and UNICEF. To provide groups with a central place for carrying on economic and other activities, multi purpose community centres are being constituted in DWCRA blocks. The cost of construction of the community centres is being met out of JRY funds and the interest earnings of the DRDA. UNICEF provides assistance for equipment and supplies upto Rs. 50,000 per centre. Additional functionaries like one Asst. project officer (women) and one additional post of Gram Sevikas has also been sanctioned (block level) the cost of which is met by UNICEF.

Achievements

There have been some improvements in rural poverty ratio which have fallen from 51.2 per cent to 40.4 per cent in 1983-84 and further to 28.7 per cent in 1991. The DWCRA programme has been implemented in 355 districts in the country. Under this programme 60,000 groups were formed and 10 lakh women have benefitted. The programme is proposed to be extended by the end of Eight Five Year Plan. For 1994-95 the central outlay for the programme is Rs. 21 crores.

Positive Features of DWCRA

This is one of the few programmes which aims at providing incomes to poor women in the rural areas.

- It provides for group formation with an accent on income generation.
- It is designed to provide supplementary employment through productive activities.
- These groups provide easier access to credit, training and other inputs.
- These groups also function as pressure groups and help their members to overcome gender barriers.
- This also provides as easy access to other services provided through government programmes iike nutrition under ICDS, literacy under the Adult education programme, health under Family Welfare programmes and access to immunisation facilities under Technology Mission.

Notwithstanding the fact that there have been successes with DWCRA in some States where experienced and committed officials took on the implementation of the programme, Overall the programme has not succeeded in establishing viable and cohesive groups. While the emphasis of DWCRA is on group approach the functionaries at the grass root level did not put in adequate time and efforts in the process of group formation. The economic activities identified for the groups were mostly traditional and stereo typed which were not productive enough to generate adequate gainful employment. Further the child development aspect which is on the label of DWCRA is missing in the content.

Keeping the experience of implementing DWCRA for a decade, following changes have been brought in the programme content:

- Thrift and credit activities are now an important part of the group forming activity. To stimulate a matching share of upto Rs. 15,000 equal to the group saving can be provided by using the budget of IRDP infrastructure.
- A pilot project of Management Information System (MIS) for DWCRA has been introduced for 19 districts in the country. The project is being fully funded by UNICEF on reimbursement basis. The total cost of the project is Rs. 8.3 lakhs. A project review committee has been constituted under the chairmanship of the Jt. Secretary of IRDP.
- For financing informal groups a pilot project was introduced in May 1990 in 16 selected districts. The informal group consist of five members and each group is entitled to revolving fund amount on pro-rata basis at Rs. 1000 per member subject to a maximum of Rs. 15,000 per group. The group is also entitled to subsidy @ 50 per cent under IRDP. The scheme was extended to 45 districts in phase II of the pilot project in 1992.
- To ensure better dovetailing of various line departments, a pilot scheme of Community Based Convergent Services (CBCS) has been started in 13 districts. The scheme for which fund was provided by UNICEF on reimbursement basis is extended to 9 more districts.

- A communication strategy has been implemented in 14 districts of the country to make planned intervention at all levels of DWCRA for better education awareness and information through mass media.

Future Strategy

Development process underwent three major shifts in the recent past reflecting in : an increased concern for the protection of environment ; an emphasis on people's participation, especially in the protection, management and regeneration of natural resources ; and the incorporation of gender concerns as an important element of development strategy.

The International conferences sponsored by the United Nations starting from the Rio through Vienna, Cairo, Copenhagen have generated a lot of interest on Social Development and highlighted the growing feminisation of poverty and possible impact on women of the structural adjustment process ; the importance of promoting equality in women's access to and participation in economic activities ; more gender-sensitive planning, policy making and implementation ; more recognition of women's current economic activities and an increase in women's access to information, skill and knowledge about economic opportunities. The problems of female migrant workers as well as of women involved in agriculture, industrial or commercial work in the formal and informal sectors have also been addressed.

- In line with the national and international concerns the women component of the mainstream poverty alleviation programmes like IRDP, DWCRA etc. should be linked and integrated with the sectoral programmes like agriculture, animal husbandry, small scale industries and forestry ;

- group approach for women should be emphasised in all poverty alleviation programmes to promote their participation and build-up of their capability.

- DWCRA programme has inherent potential to mobilise and organise women, therefore more importance should be given to it in terms of adequate staffing at grass root level with necessary training to prepare the women to form into pressure groups.

- Women should be organised into thrift and credit groups to improve their access to credit requirement and to establish creditworthiness which, in turn, would enable them to utilise institutional credit for income generation activities.

- TRYSEM training modules are to be restructured to address the managerial and entrepreneurial requirements of rural women.

- Gender specific appropriate technologies particularly in the supply of drinking water, fuel and fodder to reduce drudgery and improve productivity of women should be generated in consultation with rural women.

- Services for women under various programmes of employment, health care, family welfare, drinking water and nutrition are to be made available at grassroots level as a package through convergence and integration.

- Education of women is a critical input for improving nutritional levels, raising age at marriage, acceptance of family planning, improvement in self image and their empowerment. Special emphasis should therefore be given to non formal and adult education programmes to create conditions that will enable women to effectively participate in the educational process.

- Vocational training for women in rural areas need to be increased and linked to post training measures to set up their enterprises.

- Efforts to improve facilities in elementary schools and steps to link day care centres to primary schools can encourage girls enrolment.

- Involvement of committed NGOs in organising and training of rural women and in providing support services should be considered as an important aspect of women development programmes.

Panchayati Raj

Under the Constitution (73rd Amendment) Act, 1992, at least one-third of the total seats in panchayats at all levels are reserved for women. This applies to the posts of chairpersons also and will give women a greater say in matters of local administration at the village, block and district levels.

The Ministry of Rural Development have several schemes for providing better opportunities to the women in rural India. Apart from DWCRA, forty per cent of total assistance under IRDP and 40 per cent of trainees under TRYSEM are reserved for women. Thirty per cent of employment opportunities under JRY have also been reserved for women. Under IAY, priority is given to widows and unmarried women in allotment of houses. The elected panchayat Raj representatives at all levels should be motivated and trained so that the targets set for women development in different programmes are realised. Specifically Panchayats should take a leading role in :

1. Identification of eligible women members for different development programmes.
2. Organising women into cohesive self-help groups so that they are in a better position to participate in the programmes.
3. Providing infrastructural and physical facilities for education, health, and training and other support services to women.
4. Overseeing common resource property management so that benefits accrue to the women or women headed households.
5. Increasing access of women to inputs, services and technology to mitigate drudgery and improve their productivity.

References

1. Eighth Five Year Plan (1992-97), Vol. I & II, Govt. of India, Planning Commission, New Delhi.

2. National Perspective Plan for Women 1988-2000 AD. Report of the Core Group set up by the Deptt. of Women and Child Development, Ministry of H.R.D., Govt. of India, 1988.

3. Gender and Poverty in India. A World Bank Country Study, World Bank, Washington, D.C. 1991.

4. A State of World Rural Poverty, an enquiry into its causes and consequences, New York University Press, IFAD (1994).

5. Annual Report 1993-94, Govt. of India, Ministry of Rural Development, Deptt. of Rural Development, New Delhi.

4

Women in Development

*Avaya Kesari Parichha Pattnaik**

Ours is a male dominated society where women are described as the ' Second Sex' and the 'Second creature' who live on surplus. Their very existence has been considered as parasite on the men who rule them. Female subordination has been an essential feature of human life in all contemporary societies although with a varying degree and expression of male dominance. One of the important manifestations of this women subordination lies in the division of labour which provides a cheap and ready source of labour. Division of labour between sexes is culturally imposed and this segregated role pattern has led to a structural subordination of woman to man. However, this structural subordination of women to men has not been able to prevent them from playing a vital role in the overall development of the society. Especially, their active participation in economic activities has become common in all countries, developed and developing. But the factors affecting their participation may differ from places to places. The developed countries, many of which are now characterised by full employment, there is still room for more women in the working force. On the other hand, the developing countries which are marked by the labour surpluses, the income of the families by and large are low and the family requires the assistance of an additional earner. This economic vulnerability of the family compels their women members to go for work, supplementing the increase of income of their respective families.

In the context of women's participation in development, India projects a typical socially conservative developing country's scenario.

* Lecturer in Political Science, Aska Science College (Orissa).

Women contribute significantly to our economy, both in agricultural and non-agricultural sector. However, according to the 1971 census, though women constitute 48.2 % of our population, their participation in the economic activities is only 13 %. It is in quite contrast to the developed countries where the participation rate vary from 30 to 45 per cent. Going by the 1981 census only one-fifth of the total women are in labour force. The remaining overwhelming majority comprising of around 80 per cent, is made up of women, who are classified as non-working, because they are not economically active in the sense of participating in any economically productive activity. Of those women who work, two-thirds are engaged in full-time work whereas the other one-third are classified as marginal workers who are defined as those who have been economically active some time during the year but have not been so for the major part of the year.[1]

In the Organised Sector

The term organised sector refers to that segment of the Indian economy which offers regular employment, as for instance in the case when one is employed in corporate establishments of government offices or institutions.

Employment of Indian women in this sector has been considerably effective in getting them out of the four walls of their houses. Both big and small scale industries have given them employment apart from contributing adequately to their household earnings.

However, rapid changes in technology, automation and the curtailment of employment have drastically reduced the opportunities of women, working in organised sector. Women have suffered a setback in traditional industries such as jute, mining and cotton textiles, which were the major employers of women's labour before. The problem has become more serious by the facts that growth industries such as petrochemicals, fertilisers and engineering offer no better scope for women. Except some low technology jobs like assembling, packing, there seems to be no place for women in high technology industries.

On the other hand, there has been a noticeable trend of growth of women's employment in service sector, especially, in transportation, communication and financial institutions. Beside this, Banks, public financial institutions, insurance, posts and telegraphs and the travel and tourism industry provide better work opportunity for women. Because the service sector is open to women, with education, they also get concentrated here through the services like information handling, secretorial jobs such as typing and stenography, and clerical jobs.

Even though the organised sector offers women their best opportunity to work, the labour market in this sector is sharply segmented, with lower jobs. The division of labour in all kinds of industries involving the most modern is circumscribed by custom and tradition. The report of the committee on the status of women in India shows that out of 200 operations in the textile industry, women are employed in no more than four or five (GOI - 1974). The fact that modern technology has brought many arduous mannual jobs well within women's reach is not reflected in the actual division of labour in the industry. It is surprising that now also jobs are categorised as men's or women's on the basis of traditional norms rather than on any assesment of changes made possible by new technologies. Thus, women are now normally found in unskilled, semiskilled or low grade office jobs, or in assembling and tail-end tasks associated with packing, drilling and checking.

In the Unorganised Sector

An overwhelming presence of women are manifested in the unorganised sector, both in rural and urban areas. The National Commission on Self Employed Women estimates that 94 % of the total female work force is to be found in this sector (GOI, 1988)[2]. They participate extensively in agriculture, animal husbandry, dairing, social and agro-forestry fisheries, handicrafts,khadi and village industries, handloom weaving and sericulture. In agriculture, their activities range from sowing to weeding, transplantation and harvesting. In agro-forestry, they are engaged in the collection of minor forest produce and medicinal herbs as well as in efforstation programmes. Apart from this, women have a great deal of involvement in handloom weaving and handicrafts and in a variety of khadi and village industries. Rural area accommodates the majority of women workforce and they work in large number in homebased production and also under self-employment basis. Typically, they do work in small trades, making garments, rolling bidis and in a plethora of other activities. Women also do work in innumerable number as vendors, hawkers and domestic servants in both urban and rural segments.

The self employed women may be classified into three categories. The first are the small traders, venders and hawkers selling vegetables, fruits, eggs, household goods etc. The second are the homebased products, such as potters, milk producers, processors of agricultural products and handloom workers. The third category is made up of those who sell their labour of service (SEWA, 1988)[3].

Available statistics show that primary sector, comprising farming, livestock, forestry, fishing, plantation etc., provides work to 80 per cent of women. This includes the share of women as agricultural labourer as 51 per cent of the total women workforce.

The table -1 reflects the position of women's employment in our country.

TABLE - 1

Position of Women's Employment in the Country

Vocations	*Nos. of labour (in lakhs)*				*% of Female lab.*	
	1971		*1981*		*1971*	*1981*
	Male	*Female*	*Male*	*Female*		
1. Agriculture	1042	259	1165	365	20	24
2. Mining	8	1	11	2	11	13
3. Cottage Ind.	50	14	56	21	22	27
4. Other Ind.	99	8	158	16	7	9
5. Construction	20	2	32	4	9	10
6. Transport & Commerce	95	5	130	9	5	7
7. Trade & Com.	43	1	59	2	2	3
8. Others	135	28	154	32	15	16
Total	1491	313	1775	450	17	20

Source : 'Bharater Jatiya Aay', M. Mukherjee, P. 177.

Available statistics also give us the information that the percentage share of women in total labour force is 29 per cent. Their share in agriculture 62 per cent, in industry 11 per cent and in service sector it is 27 per cent. As for the data of the table there has been an increasing in the participation of women in all sectors. But the increase in cottage industries and agriculture who was higher incomparison to the rest.

Tribal Women

Some recent studies indicate that in the tribal world women contribute to the working force in a more substantial way than the non-tribal world. Precisely, in the Indian context, the forces of modernisation at work in the tribal socities have produced a two-fold tread. They have created conditions for proliferation of occupation for tribal women. It has been noticed that more and more tribal women now move from the primary sector to the secondary and tertiary sectors of employment. With opening of new vistas of opportunities of working at mines and various industries in tribal areas large number of women have been drawn into occupations hitherto unknown to them. On account of working of multiple factors like growing industrialisation, growth of education and the impact of Christianity, opportunities for diversification of occupation as well as social mobility among the tribal women have multiplied. The building up of roads and development of fast communications have led to a large number of tribal women taking to petty trading, causal labour work and other commercial activities in some parts of the country.

'While the ratio between male and female workers in the general population of the country is 5:1, it is 3:1 among the tribal people.' Among the non-tribal women 11:9 per cent are workers where as 20.75 per cent are workers in the tribal women segment.[4]

The comparative figures of the participation rate of the non-tribal and tribal workers in the different sectors of economy are shown in table - 2.

The available statistics also show that since the tribal economy is largely confined to the primary sector, 90.6% of the tribal female workers are engaged in agriculture as cultivators or as labourers, 2.6% in pastoralism, hunting etc. and 0.6% in mining and quarring.

TABLE - 2

Primary Sector

Occupational categories	*Culti- vation*	*Agricultural labourers*	*Mining*	*Livestock, Forestry, Fishing, Hunting etc.*
General female	29.8%	50.5%	0.4%	2.5%
Tribal female	42.7%	48.9%	0.6%	2.6%

Secondary Sector

Occupational categories	*Household Industries*	*Manufacturing etc.*	*Construction*
General female	4.3%	2.8%	0.7%
Tribal female	1.3%	0.9%	0.3%

Tertiary Sector

Occupational categories	*Trade & Commerce*	*Transport etc.*	*Other services*
General female	1.8%	0.5%	-
Tribal female	0.6%	0.2%	-

* *Source* : S.S. Prasad, 'Tribal Women Labourers', p. 3.

However, the traditional tribal economy which rested mainly on agriculture is no longer the only source of income for them. In other words the tribal economy is no longer exclusively agricultural. Profit from trading and industrial work also began and the tribal economy of late cruising towards becoming more marcantile and industrial.

In areas where a lot of constructional activity is being carried out such as, in industrial areas in Bihar, Madhya Pradesh, and Orissa, tribal women are lifted on trucks from the tribal villages and nearabouts by the contractors. In the evening they are usually taken back to their respective villages. In some cases the tribal women even migrate outside their villages, district and state to some distant places for several months for working in the brick-kilns, agricultural fields, tea-Estates etc. Direct involvement of tribal women in this short of activities not only help in making better their own standard of living but also it makes a positive contribution to the overall socio-economic development of that area. Tribal women also feel inclined to go in for such short and long term employment avenues because it provides them ready cash which they prefer spending on clothes, new fashion ornaments, and other items of daily use. Besides the monetary gains, they also cherish the pleasure of daily outing which is actively associated with such occupations.[5]

Rural Working Women

The structural subordination of women to men becomes more manifested when the phenomenon is considered in the context of the rural working women. The rural working women present themselves as an unavoidable lot. "They work in the scorching sun and in the pouring rain. Away from the home they slog breaking the stones at quarries and doing all drudgery at the mines, factory premises, brick-kilns etc. They earn on their own and supplement the family income to keep off starvation." The rural women have excelled in many ways in comparison to their male counterparts. They do many things more than the men do. Apart from performing all their day to day activities like cooking and looking after children, they go around to fetch grass and fodder in order to keep the fire of hearth glowing. They even operate the wells in order to irrigate the land. They sow the seeds, transplant and harvest the crops. 'This is the story of the millions of workers in India's 5,60,000 villages, the unknown soldiers who help keep our economy going, keep the burns to the full and help India occupay one of the premier places by engineering the Green Revolutions.

Following table - 3 gives us the information about participation of main workers, both male and female in 1971 and 1981.

TABLE - 3

Work Participation of Main Workers, 1971-81

All Ages	*Males*		*Females*	
	1971	*1981*	*1971*	*1981*
Total	52.61	52.66	12.06	13.99
Rural	53.62	52.62	13.06	16.00
Urban	48.40	48.54	6.35	7.28

* *Source* : Census of India, 1981.

As for the data available work participation rate of male workers remain unchanged during 1971-81 but participation rate of female workers increased from 12 in 1971 to nearly 14 in 1981. In rural areas, work participation rate of female workers slightly declined but female work participation rate rose from 13 to 16. The overall participation rate of women went up more sharply than those of men over this decade. There was an increase in the participation of women to men working as agricultural labourers (Banerjee, 1989, P. 14). Thus the 1971-81 decade was marked by a noticeable increase in the number of women rural workers. Their share in the rural workforce went up nearly one-third of the total work force.[6]

In Science and Technology

Indian women are no longer lagging behind on the once considered 'tough' subjects like science, technology, Engineering and Medicine. They are fast advancing in the so called male dominated world in understanding and mastering the intricacies involved in exploring the frontiers of science. They have excelled themselves even in the interdisciplinary areas such as Bio-physics, Biochemistry, Biotechnology, Micro electronics, Computerscience and management etc., contributing not only to the advancement of science but also towards the socio-economic progress of the country. The work of Dr. (Mrs.) Hinduja of Bombay in the birth of test tube babies is just one of the innumerable examples of Indian women's scientific excellence.

In the academic front, opportunities to women for persuing higher education at the graduate, postgraduate levels are provided at all the universities and technical colleges across the country ever since the independence. The highly specialised and professional courses offered by the academic institutions are no longer the exclusive prerogative of men folk.

According to the statisticians, world's third largest scientific and technical manpower exhists in India and 30 lakh technical personnel are working in the R & D organisations in the country. It becomes a matter of pride that out of this 10%, that is 3 lakh, are women. Statistics also show that women's enrollment in the fields of science and technology was 8.2% of the total enrollment of 4,80,000 during 1992-93. There has been a remarkable increase in the number of women enrolled in the institutions of higher education from 40,000 to 15 lakhs, their percentage in total enrollment has increased from 7 in 1987 to 33 in 1992-93. An interesting feature is that among women enrolled in the science and technology faculities, 13.6% belong to medicine, 8.3% to pure science and 4.8% to Engineering.[7]

An interesting feature is that the number of women taking of the Engineering courses has increased from 1% in 1975 to about 10% in 1990, making it the largest as far as the centre of work is concerned where 30% of engineers employed in the national institutions are women. This is followed by Civil-Services (22%), Public Sector (19%), Private Sector (13%) and 10% each in private sector (small) and government R & D sector respectively. Among the states Kerala has the largest number of women engineers followed by Tamilnadu and Karnataka, Maharashtra, Andhra Pradesh, Gujarat, Delhi, Madhya Pradesh, West Bengal and Uttar Pradesh.[8]

Many positive steps have been taken in our country to make women's role in development better understood and appreciated. The introduction of the scheme 'science and technology for women' in the 6th five year plan is a recognitation of women as an integral part of national development. It focuses on development strategies to reduce the drudgery of women by the application of science and technology.

However, it is a matter of great concern that although women constitute about half of India's population they have made a small representation in the S & T field. Thus, there is an urgent need to developed the scientific and technical capabilities of women in large numbers in order to make them equal partners in the overall development of the country. And this has to be followed by proper projection of the significant contribution of the women technocrates in order to attract other women to take up professionals in the technical fields.

Conclusion

The discussion has made it clear that the role of a women does not complete by just becoming our's daughter, sister, mother or wife. She has got to play a more significant role apart from this traditional multidimensional character for the betterment of mankind. As regards the role of women in the development of our country it has been calculated that a 1971 prices the contributions of women labour to the Net National Income where rupees 4962 and 7574 crores in 1971 and 1981 respectively, in percentages from it was 12.4 in 1971 and 16 in 1981. This data doesn't take into account the contributions made by women by way of their working in the house-hold management. If we make the calculation by including the income generated by the women between the age group of 15 to 44 (in terms of opportunity costs) than the total contribution of the women labour to the N.N.I. will be Rs. 17,322 and Rs. 22,474 crores in 1971 and 1981 respectively and in percentage term they will be 37 in 1971 and 36 in 1981.[9]

Regardless of the contribution made by women towards the development of the country, no substantial change has taken place in the socio-economic status. Bare facts and statistical figure reveal more than loquacious speaches and valuable writings on the status of women. There has been a decline in the sex ratio over the decades - from 970 in 1901 to 927 in 1991 (sex ratio in India is the number of females to 1000 makes). When male figures are indexed at 100, females stand at 93 in population, 55 in literacy, 34 on years of schooling and 41 on labour force.[10] According to the 1991 census, the percentage of male literacy in the country was 64.13%, where as the female literacy was 39.29%.

The above mentioned facts and figures reveal the still existing inequality between man and women in the Indian socio-economic life. One of the ways to ensure gender equality is the empowerment of women. The government's strategy for the empowerment of women has been to reserve seats for women in education, in employment and most important of all in the Panchayati Raj institutions, so that women are effectively able to participate in democratic decision making process. Our Parliament represented a record higher 8.1% of women parliamentarians during the Eighth Lok Sabha elections.

However there is denying the fact that women in our days have begun to acquire the status of equality with man and several arena till recently closed for women have opened their gates to them. Nevertheless the struggle for complete emancipation and equality goes on.

We worshipped goddess Durga as our mother, accepted Mrs.

Indira Gandhi as our leader but forgot about millions of our daughters and sisters who contributed immensely to the development of our country by living unnoticed in the remote rural and in accessible hill areas. Would they remain forever as 'unsung heroines, born to die in the back-yard of human civilization, carrying on the burden of humanity for a mere pittance?'

Reference

1. Leela Gulati : 'Women in the Unorganised Sector With Special Reference to Kerala', Women and Work in India, Edited by A.N. Sharma and Seema Singh (Indian Societies of Labour Economics And B.R. Publishing Corporations - Delhi)

2. Uma Ramaswamy : 'Women and Development'. Women and Work in India. Edited by A.N. Sharma and Seema Singh.

3. *Ibid.*

4. Sushama Sahaya Prasad : 'Tribal Women Labourers : Aspects of Economic and Physical Exploitations.' (Gian Publishing House - Delhi).

5. *Ibid.*

6. Bhagwan Singh and Seema Singh : 'Planning and the Plight of Female Rural Labourers in India, 'Women and Work in India.

7. Pawan Sikka : ' Women in Science and Technology, 'Yojana, Jan. 15, 1995.

8. *Ibid.*

9. P.C.Dey : 'Women's Employment and its Role in The Development of North-Eastern India : A Case Study,' 'Vision', Vol : IX, No. 182.

10. Human Resource Development Report - 1994.

5

Tribal Women and Their Participation in Developmental Activities

*S.K. Sahu**

Various studies refer to the fact of marginalisation of women in all sector despite the proclamation of gender equality in different legal and constitutional provisions. The pressence and participation of women in formal democratic process is woefully inadequate at all the levels - social, economic and political. This paper seeks to analyse the extent and pattern of political mobilisation among the tribal women - a social category characterised by low corporate socio-economic status in a context punctuated by wide spread participation. Their low effectiveness and their numerically less orientations for social- economic and political efficacy constitute the premise of this study.

Tribal Situation in India

The term 'tribe' was first used by the colonial administration for designating the primitive communities with distinctive language and culture. Here, the primitive communities denotes low growth rate, pre-industrial level of technology, extremely low level of literacy and an absense of literate tradition. Their world view is dominated by animism, animatism, naturism, totemism, shammanism and occultism. They are believed to be the autochthones or early-settlers of the country, and hence are referred to as 'Adivasis'. They are also designated as 'Vanyajati' as they are usually inhabit in forest, hilly, mountainous terrain, undulating plateau and inaccessible tracts.

* Lecturer in Political Science, Khemundi College, Orissa

India has longest concentration of tribals in the world next to Africa. As per 1991 census, they number 67.76 million accounting for 8.01% of India's population. About 80% of them live in remote forest areas with no access to modern socio-economic inputs. They constitute aboriginal elements in Indian society. It is difficult to define the tribal peoples in India in terms of any single set of formal criteria. Within various tribal areas there arc ethonographs variations in terms.

The tribal people, better known as the 'Scheduled Tribes' are in majority in more than 329 Taluks, on the basis of 50% of the ST population, areas have been identified in the country. In such areas more than 65% of their total population lives. It means that the tribal people are the dominant groups in some areas. In Nagaland, Megalaya, Arunachal Pradesh and Mizoram, majority of the population being to Scheduled Tribes. They are found in relatively a big number in Madhya Pradesh, Orissa, Bihar, Assam and Uttar Pradesh. In Madhya Pradesh along more than one crore tribals are found. According to the Scheduled Tribe lists Modification order 1956, there are 414 different tribes on the various States of India. So far as the numerical strength is concerned, the tribal communities range all the way from the Santhals, the Gonds and the Bhils whose number exceeds 4 million each, to small groups like the Mankindia numbering less than 1,000 or the Chance numbering less than 100. Thus a high level of social cultural expression co-exists with the poverty, starvation, deprivation, illiteracy, ignorance and isolation in tribal India.

Post-Independence Approach

With independence came a great awakening in this country. The welfare state gave due recognition to the status and suffering of the tribal-folk who had suffered from neglect, isolation, exploitation, inferiority complex, discrimination, degradation and socio-economic backwardness for centuries and remained far behind the national mainstream. The political leadership, Indian Constitution and Government adopted various measures to protect and promote the interests of the tribal population. Over the years there has been a host of legislations and welfare programmes for protection and economic development of the tribals. On the whole, the central objective of national policy for the tribals has been their socio-economic progress with a view to integrating them with the rest of the population on a footing of equality while maintaining their cultural autonomy to the largest extent possible. There has been a constant search for a strategy which will effect a planned change balancing their distinctive natural talent, cultural forms, value systems and personality traits with the imperatives of growth and modernisation. The objective of the state policy is thus to work through their socio-cultural institutions putting right emphasis on the ecology of the region and taking into account the tribals dependence on their natural habits.

The great national leaders like Mahatma Gandhi, Jawaharlal Nehru, Takkar Bapa, Bhimrao Ambedkar and many others who fought with the British for India's independence had expressed their concern for the betterment and integration of the tribals into the national mainstream in terms of equality and social justice. This has found expression in the Constitution of India. The Constitution provides various concessions and safeguards to the tribal people. These provisions have led to the development of an administrative structure suitable for protecting the interests of the tribal people and acclerating the pace of their socio-economic modernization. Now the Union and State Governments, non-Government agencies, voluntary agencies, social workers, religious agencies, and academic agencies are actively engaged in the field of tribal welfare.

Thus the post-independence approach rejected the pre-independence British policy of segregation and sought for assimilation and integration of the tribals with the rest of the nation. Huge amounts have been spent for implementing various welfare schemes for the tribals. As a result the tribals are now passing through a phase of development with the rest of the country.

The assimilation of the tribal people with rest of the population which is the present approach, is a continuous process and the culture contact with the neighbouring nontribals is responsible for this. In India the tribals have come in contact with Hindu and other communities since the ages. They have different degrees of culture contacts leading to various degrees of assimilation in different parts of this country. While some tribals have accepted Hindu Culture, others have accepted Christianity, Buddhism and Islamic faiths. Many authorities have tried to classify the tribals according to their level of integration with rest of the Indian people and culture. According to Majumdar, the tribes can be classified as ; (i) assimilated and (ii) adaptive or transitional. The transitional groups are in three successive stages viz, (a) commensalic (economic ties with neighbours) (b) symbiotic (interdependence) and (c) acculturative.

Elwin and Dube have given fourfold and fivehold classifications respectively. The Tribal Welfare Committee under Indian Conference of Social Work (1952) classified the tribes into following four main divisions.

(1) Isolated and homogenous communities still retaining their distinctive life-styles.
(2) Semi-Tribal communities living in close interaction with the peasant communities in rural areas.
(3) Acculturated Communities migrated to urban areas, taken up occupations and adopted the culture traits of the urban community.
(4) Totally assimilated tribals.

Roy Burman (1971) had given a fourfold classification in respect of their extent of Hinduization.

(1) Incorporated in the Hindu social order.
(2) Positively oriented towards Hindu social orders.
(3) Negatively oriented towards Hindu social orders.
(4) Indifferent towards Hindu social order.

Considering from all angles i.e. extent of Hinduization, degree of acculturation and level of socio-economic development Vidyarthi (1976) has assessed the level of integration of the tribals as per the following five-fold divisions.

(1) **Distinct Tribal Communities :** Living in highly isolated regions e.g. forest hunting tribes and shifting cultivators.
(2) **Rural Tribes** : Who are living in rural areas and are dependent on agriculture and other allied pursuits. e.g. agriculturist tribes.
(3) **Semi-Acculturated Tribals :** Who have successfully blended their own agricultural traditions with the

neighbouring people and the situation e.g., the tribal communities living in mixed villages.

(4) **Acculturated Tribals :** Who have adopted modern occupations in urban and industrial settings and have mixed to a great extent with the rest of the population e.g., the urbanities and industrial workers.

(5) **Totally Assimilated Tribals :** Who have acquired a place in the Hindu caste system e.g., the Raj Gonds, the Bhumija, the Majhis, the Khasas etc.

Concept of Tribal Modernisation

Tribal modernisation is a process denoting a change in the traditional or quasi-traditional role-structure of the tribal communities and consequently promoting a dual system of values for self and societal transformation, towards a certain desired form of social structure, values and norms. Here, categorisation of social structures, values or norms into modern or traditional should not raise a host of theoretical problems. Because it is assumed that structures and allied forms, values and norms associated with modern, developed or advanced societies are modern and those associated with the underdeveloped or tribal societies are traditional. Another question which one may raise is of priority at individual and social levels in the realm of modernization. This problem has been summed up by Myron Weiner in his observation that some scholars suggest that starting point of any definition of modernization is not in the character of the society but in the character of individuals.

In the broad sphere of Indian society, the representation of tribes is although numerically small but culturally, it is significant and effective. The tribal heritage consists of many valuable ingredients of Indian culture. Hence, a proper identification of these ingredients is essential to explore the real nature of Indian social system and cultural heritage. This may provide a sound base for the study of modernisation of Indian society. Similarly, the tribals exhibit a variety of customs and traditions typical of their own life styles.

The socio-cultural transformation of tribal societies has occurred more rapidly in recent times. Tribal societies have not remained immune to change. This is because of the break of a certain degree of isolation and subsequent growth of cultural contact. The transformation has been generally channelised through the phenomenon and by some other processes, such as Sanskritization, acculturation, etc. Because of these forces and processes, as also for differentiation in customary ways of various groups, the uniformity in tribal socio-cultural milieu has been disrupted.

Studies have revealed that by urbanisation entirely new elements are introduced in the socio-cultural set-up of the tribes. The increasing urban contact with a stronger or superior culture are established and are gradually becoming firm. Technological developments are steadily penetrating the regions surrounded by an urban centre. The urban centre functions as foci of diffusion of innovations. Due to the contact and diffusion of innovations, metamorphosis of the economic and socio cultural fabric of a traditional society starts taking place. As a result, money economy gradually tends to replace barter economy, charactersing the transition phase of urbanised transformation. Finally, the process of cultural liquidation gains momentum eroding the age-old regional cultural set-up and accelerates the modernisation. In fact, these marked changes in the tribal communities can be broadly categorised into three stages, from the transformative view point:

(i) Some tribes have sufficiently changed (modernisation stage).
(ii) Some are in transition (adoption stage).
(iii) Some still remain fogged down within the frame of traditionally (latency state).

"The conflict formulations of tribal modernization are based on the theme of tribal exploitation and on the emergency of consciousness of relative deprivation in the areas of economic, political, civic and educational spheres of tribal life. Here, the ideology is treated as the basic motivational force for the movements, consequently modern strategies and the process of modernization are adopted to mobilise group support. It has been assumed that the traditional process in the past was originally responsible for inititating changes in tribal societies. It was accelerated by the modern process. If the first process brought forth a Hindu model before the tribals, the Western urban, Industrial, democratic model for inducing transformation.

In essence, "the transformation and the interaction of tribal culture with it, offers fascinating field of research for social scientists. It is, therefore, suggested that a comparative study of socio-cultural transformation of tribal and non-tribal societies with identical environmental conditions and under similar urban impact, may provide a key to ascertain the role-differential cultural back-ground of the modernization process."

Tribal Women in Development

Women have a significant role in tribal economy and society. The total tribal popuiation in India is about 63 million. While the ratio of male and female workers to the general population of the country is 5:1, it is 3:1 for the tribal population. Among the non-tribal women 11.9 per cent are workers, and among tribal women 20.75 per cent are workers.

The status of tribal women witnessed a downship in the decades of the recent past. Tribal women played a very important role in farming through their active participation in shifting cultivation. The arrival of settled farming has marginalised their role. Tribal women also contributed a lot to the family through food-gathering but this role has also been cut short due to degradation of forests. Thus their economic status has come down. Their social status also has witnessed a downfall due to the influence of non-tribals and Hinduism on the tribal society.

Tribal women play a crucial role in development due to their direct and greater participation in tribal economy. Their interactions with forests and the traditional ways in which they manage natural resources, harvesting significant amounts without depleting the resources, make their role in sustainable development more prominent than that of tribal menflok. Their instinctive efforts in conservation and judicious use of nature's wealth makes their role all the more important at a time when environmental problems are threatening to put the future of humanity in peril. Therefore, tribal women are being given more responsibilities in social forestry schemes, conservation projects and wasteland development.

Despite erosion in the recent past, the social status of tribal women is much higher than that of their non-tribal counterparts. Tribal women belonging to most tribal groups are free to select their life-partners and also seek and obtain divorce if they are not happy with their husband. Widow remarriage is also allowed. Further, the deplorable dowry system is not practiced in tribal society which the bridegroom has to pay money to the parents of the girl he wants to marry.

Though some tribal societies do not allow women to participate in religious ceremonies, tribal women enjoy several other liberties which their non-tribal counterparts cannot even think of. In tribal societies women are the managers of the house. Cooking and providing food for the family members, ensuring drinking water supply and keeping the house are activities which non-tribal women also do. In addition to these, tribal women collect fuelweed, fodder for cattle and edible fruits, tubers, etc., to supplement the staple family food. In the case of tribes who practise shifting cultivation, women do the sowing and harvesting while men take charge of clearing the forest and allied activities.

In general, tribal women work harder than their menfolk, putting in more hours and taking up more responsibilities. Even after industrialisation and the resultant commercialisation crept into tribal economy, women continued to play a significant role. Collection of minor forest produce is done mostly by women and children. Many tribal women also work as labourers in industries, households and the construction industry, contributing vitally to their family income. Despite exploitation by contractors and managers, tribal labourers are more sincere and honest than non-tribal labourers.

Since the political and social life of tribals is closely and intricately linked. The political status of tribal women moved in accordance with their social status. However, the political status of women was not as important as that of tribal men, even in the past. The tribal chief, village leader and the like were all men. Most, if not all, of the village panchayat members were also men. The Union Government and various State Governments have taken steps, including legal action, to include women in village panchayats. However, this has not brought about any major change in the political status of tribal women.

The custom of bride-price among the tribes is based on the

recognition of the importance of women's role in the economic sphere. It is the reflection of the fact of the woman being a productive worker in the economy of the tribe. In case a women leaves her home after marriage the parents are deprived of a productive worker. They also lose the assistance of a son-in-law if the residence is not matrilocal. Bride-price is, therefore, said to be a compensation for this loss to the parents. The bride-price can be in the form of cash or kind. It can also be in the exchange of sisters to some other female relative for a wife is a variation of the same thing. All these different forms are found among the tribes of India.

Diversified Women Activities

Khasis are a materialineal tribe in north-east India. It has been observed that there are certain occupations which are exclusively in the hands of Khasi females. These are selling of fish, stitched cloth and supply of tea and snacks in the offices, etc. The Khasis practice both shifting and wet paddy cultivation. Along with these two types of agricultural practices they also grow potato, orange, pineapple, betelnut and betel-leaf. In these activities women cultivators and women agricultural labourers are numerically more than male.

In other activities concerning livestock, plantation, construction, household industry and other services, women are present in considerable percentages. (1) In Khasi society women take an active part in trade which elsewhere is usually in the hands of men ; (2) many women maintain their families by engaging in different type of occupations such as sewing clothes, selling fish, supply of tea and snacks, etc., and (3) there are many women petty traders who shift from one occupation to another within a short span of time.

Industrialisation and its harmful side-effects have changed the life of tribals in a drastic way and made them face disastrous situations. Industrialists have plundered the resource base of tribals, resulting in displacement of tribals and a lamentable fall in the quality of their life. Tribal women have been the worst sufferers since they now have to work much harder in search of water, fuelwood, fodder, edible fruits and tubers, and other MFP. All this has put them in a difficult situation. Several organisations have launched programmes for the upliftment of tribal women. The situation is witnessing a slow but steady change.

Education, health care and vocational training have to be imparted to tribal women to improve the quality of their lives. Also their traditional rights over minor forest products has to be restored. Exploitation of tribal women labour must also stop. Efforts are being made by the governmental and non-governmental organisations to achieve this end.

The Christian tribes have followed the path of directed change. Women have moved into non-traditional occupations. Since the church always encourages thrift, one often finds women have been able to put aside their extra earnings as savings instead of spending it on luxury goods. Some have used it in acquiring property in their own names particularly among the Protestants. Tribal Christian women participate in large number in the modern political structure of the country. Irrespective of their religious affiliation, the tribal people have come under the generalised forces of modernisation in recent years. It is expected that with the growth of awareness of the special privileges and programmes meant for them, they will be in a position to utilise these more fruitifully and it will be easier for the coming generation of tribal women to participate in the development programmes. However, the broad policy framework for organising poor unorganised tribal women can be forwarded in the following lines.

Policy Thrust

Women should be provided proper training and skill for their economic well-being. Sericulture has been suited for tribal women as one of the enterprises, with high potential for employment and income.

There is a need for transforming the traditional values, social dogmas, superstitions, illiteracy through the provision of social awareness programmes and proper education for skill development.

Regional planning should be made for tribal women on the basis of their needs, abilities, acceptability, attitude, feasibility. In all such plans, community participation and involvement of rural unorganised women is indispensable.

References

1. Bose, N.K., *Tribal Life in India*, NBT, 1971.

2. Das Gupta, P.K. Impact of Industrialisation on a Tribal South Bihar - India. *Current Authropology*, Vol.17, No.1, 1976.

3. K. Ajay, "Tribal Development, Government Efforts and Performances" Third Concept, Vol. 8, Aug. 1994.

4. Jain, Devika, Women's Quest for Power. Vikas Publishing House Pvt. Ltd., Ghaziabad, 1980

5. M. Krishna, "Bonds Women Role Status Analysis", *Indian Anthropoligist* Vol.12 (2), 1982.

6. Sachidananda, "Social Structure, Status and Mobility Pattern ; the Case of Tribal Women", *Man in India*, Vol. 158 (1), Jan. - March, 1978.

7. San. J., "Tribal Women and Rural Development", Research Project sponsored by ICSSR, NASSDDC.

8. Shashi, S.S., *The Gaddi Tribe of Himachal Pradesh*, Sterling Publishers, Delhi 1977.

9. Singh, J.P. and Vyas, N.N. and Mann, R.S., *Tribal Women and Development*, M L V Tribal Research Institute, Udaipur, 1988.

6

Occupation and Educational Change of Tribal Women of Assam : A Case Study

*Dr. Pranay Jyoti Goswami**

This chapter aims at discussing the extent of transition that has taken place in the sphere of occupation and education of the Scheduled Tribe women population of Barak Valley region of Assam during post-independence period.

Geographical Profile of the Study

The Barak Valley region of Assam comprises the districts of Cachar, Hailakandi and Karimganj. It is compeletely separated from the plains of Brahamaputra Valley by North Cachar Hills district of Assam and Jaintia Hills district of Meghalaya. It is a small plain bounded on the North by the North Cachar Hills and Jaintia Hills, on the South by Mizo Hills, on the East by the state of Manipur and is contagious to the Sylhet district of Bangladesh on the West. The valley is situated between the longitudes 92° 15' E and 93° 15' E and the latitudes 24° 8' N and 25° 8' N.

Population

The Principal linguistic community in the Barak Valley is the Bengalees. The communities other than the Bengalees are the Meitei

* Lecturer in Economics, Silchar, Assam.

Manipuri, Bisnupriya (Manipuri), the Kuki, the Naga, the Khasi, the Barmans, the Tipra, the Assamese, the Hmar and the Nepalis etc. Tea garden labourers of tribal origin e.g. the Oraon, the Munda, the Hoe, the Santhal etc. have been residing in the valley. The total population of the valley as per 1991 census was 2491496. District wise population by scheduled caste and scheduled Tribe is shown in Table-1.

TABLE - 1

SC and ST Population in Barak Valley (1991).

		Scheduled Caste		*Scheduled Tribe*	
Districts	*Total Population*	*Number*	*P.C. to total population*	*Number*	*P.C. to total population*
Cachar	1215385	178624	14.69	16563	1.36
Hailakandi	449048	54107	12.04	715	.159
Karimganj	827063	120602	14.58	1430	.172
Barak Valley	2491496	353333	14.18	18708	.751

Source : Compiled by the author on the basis of census reports of 1991.

About ninety nine percent of the Scheduled Tribe population of the Barak Valley lives in the rural areas. The Barmans are the only scheduled Tribe population in the Valley. They are a section of the Kachari tribe and rules in plains of Cachar for about 230 years. According to Edward Gait,[1] an eminent historian, the Kacharis extended their rule in the plains of Cachar around 1603 A.D. They ruled roughly till British annexation of Cachar in 1832.

Method of Date Collection

The primary data required were collected from the Heads of the Barman families by direct personal interview with the help of interview schedules previously framed with an eye to the objectives of the study. Secondary data were collected from various Government departments, Official Agencies and Organisation,. Observation method and group discussion were also adopted.

Field Investigation

The preliminary field investigation was done during the period from October 1985 to October 1986. Feild study was also made thereafter a number of times as and when it was felt necessary.

Reference Period

The study was undertaken relating to the year 1984-85, though the information was collected for the period since independence as far as possible.

Limitation of the Data

The Barman households seldom maintain any written records. The respondents replied the queries from the memory. It is obvious that information furnished in that manner suffers from certain limitation. In regard to secondary data the most important limitation has been imposed by the absence of 1981 census in assam due to unusual political conditions then prevailing.

Design

For the present study multi-stage sampling method is adopted. At the first stage sampling unit, one district, i.e. Cachar out of two districts, namely, Cachar and Karimganj in the Barak Valley[2] is purposely selected because there is a very negligible number of Scheduled Tribe Population in Karimganj district. Then the enlisted areas comprising of Scheduled Tribe population as recorded in the District Census Handbook, 1971, Cachar district was noted for the purpose of investigation work ; but the investigation, (it must be noted), establishes that some villages do have Scheduled Tribe do not in fact contain any such population. On the other hand the investigation also revealed that there are still other villages which are not shown to have any scheduled Tribe Community to have tribal Population. Accordingly, while we have included the latter type of villages within the scope of this study, the former type has, obviously, been excluded. Excepting barely few, all the Scheduled Tribe population living in the Cachar district happen to belong to the Barman Community. Conveniently, these villages have been grouped into four categories on the basis of their ethnic composition, as shown below :

(i) Tribal Villages	:	A village in which Tribal population is more than 75 per cent of the total population.
(ii) Predominantly Tribal Village	:	A village in which Tribals constitute 50 per cent to 75 percent of the total population.
(iii) Mixed village	:	A village in which Tribels constitute 25 per cent to 50 per cent of the total population.
(iv) Predominantly non-Tribal village	:	A village in which Tribal population is 25 per cent or less of the total population.

I have been found that those predominantly non tribal villages which have tribal population of less than 10 per cent of the total are the ones where respondents are rarely available. Due to this, these villages have been excluded from investigation.

In the second stage, at least 25 per cent sample villages are taken from each group. The following considerations have been made for the selection of the sample villages:

(i) The villages are selected in such away that all the police stations (as per 1971 census) where the Barmans have been residing are well represented.

(ii) The sample villages include interior as well as roadside villages.

(iii) The sample villages include tribal, predominantly tribal, mixed and predominantly non-tribal villages.

In the third stage, the number of tribal families residing in each sample village was then ascertained after discussion with the village headman or other prominent person of the village. The tribal population under study are in general, occupationally agriculturist. Their living is to be wedded to other types of occupations like industry, whitecolar jobs etc. However, there are a few isolated cases of households among which some members have been found to be engaged in occupation other than agriculture. Accordingly, households have been stratified on the basis of land holdings namely (i) Landless (no land), (ii) The marginal (.01-2.5 acres), (iii) Small (2.51 to 5 acres), (iv) Medium (5.01 Acres – 10 Acres), and (v) the big farms (10.01 Acres and above). A proportional number of households from each group are selected in such a way that 25. p.c. of the total Barman households come within the purview of our sample. The name of the selected villages and total number of sample households are given in Table 2 which will show that the personal investigation took into account 19 sample villages with 195 households and population of 1139.

TABLE - 2

Name of the Selected Villages Under Survey

Sl. No.	*Name of Village*	*Type of Village*	*Name of G.P.*	*Police Station*	*Total No. of Barman Houses*	*Total No. of Sample House-hold*
1	2	3	4	5	6	7
1.	Dhanipur Forest Village	T.V.	Bhaga Bazar	Dhalai	64	16
2.	Joypur Pt-III (Langracherra)	T.V.	Joypur	Lakhipur	67	17
3.	Chailthacherra	T.V.	Kashpur	Udarbond	54	13
4.	Dharamnagar	T.V.	Harinagar	Lakhipur	38	10
5.	Lakhinagar Forest Village-I	T.V.	Jiri Fulertal	Jirighat	77	19
6.	Gorervitor	P.T.V.	Bikrampur	Katigarah	44	11
7.	Kacharigaon (Changrapur)	P.T.V.	Jhatinga	Borkhola	20	5
8.	Kumacherra	P.T.V.	Harinagar	Lakhipur	101	25
9.	Koorkari Pt-II	M.V.	Kalain	Katigarh	40	10

(Contd.)

TABLE - 2 (contd.)

1	2	3	4	5	6	7
10.	Bijoypur	M.V.	Jhatinga	Borkhala	30	8
11.	Gonganagar-VI	M.V.	Bhuban Hill	Sonai	43	11
12.	Thaligram	M.V.	Khaspur	Udarbond	54	13
13.	Gonganagar-I	M.V.	Bhuban Hill	Sonai	32	8
14.	Bilaipur	M.V.	Niz-Barnarpur	Lala	55	14
15.	Dalugram	P.T.V.	Jhatinga	Borkhala	13	3
16.	Siberbond	P.N.T.V.	Khaspur	Udarbond	24	6
17.	Harinagar	P.N.T.V.	Harinagar	Lakhipur	8	2
18.	Laburbond	P.N.T.V.	Dudpatil	Silchar	8	2
19.	Pachim Mutracherra	P.N.T.V.	Harinagar	Lakhipur	7	2

** T.V. = Tribal Village, P.T.V. = Predominantly Tribal Village, M.V = Mixed Village, P.N.T.V. = Predominantly Non-Tribal Village.

Occupational Diversification Among the Barman Women

During British period the Barmans maintained their livelihood by hunting, fishing, hill agriculture and plain agriculture. After independence, because of settlement of many immigrants of Bangladesh in the hilly lands and also because of Govt. Policy, they have been compelled to give up shifting cultivation (Jhum) and are now maintaining their livelihood mainly from settled cultivation. In the different stages of agricultural operation, both man and women work together. Census reports of 1961 and 1971 throw light on the occupational pattern of tribal population. 1981 census was not conducted in Assam because of unusual political situation then prevailing. The data regarding occupational pattern of individual tribal population as per 1991 cansus has not yet been published. The occupational distribution appearing in the census report may conveniently be arranged in the following classification :

(i) *Primary Sector :* Person engaged in cultivation, agricultural labour and other farming activities like livestock, forestry, plantation etc. belong to this group.

(ii) *Secondary Sector :* Persons engaged in mining and quarrying manufacturing and construction belong to this group.

(iii) *Teretiary Sector :* Persons engaged in the Trade, Commerce transport, stroage and other services are included in this sector.

Sectorwise, occupational classification of Scheduled Tribes of the Valley in 1961 and 1971 is appended in the Table 3.

TABLE - 3

Sector-wise Occupational Classification of the Scheduled Tribe (Rural) in 1961 and 1971.

Category	*Percentage of Scheduled Tribe to Total Scheduled Tr. Worker*					
	1961			*1971*		
	M	*F*	*T*	*M*	*F*	*T*
Primary	94.46	56.9	77.2	85.6	43.9	81.5
Secondary	.54	42.4	19.7	2.2	48.9	6.8
Tertiary	5.9	.67	3.1	12.2	7.2	11.7

Source : Computed by the author on the basis of the following Census Report.

Census of India, 1961, Vol. III, part V a, page 186.
Census of India, 1971, Assam, Series 3, part II-c (i)
Social and Cultural Tables, page 10-11

Table-3, demonstrates that in 1961 there were negligible percentage of female (.67) in the tertiary sector. This was due to their abysmally low level of educational attainment during this period. In the secondary sector, female work participation was higher than their counterparts during 1961 and 1971. This high participation of women among Barmans was due to the fact that they were mainly engaged in the traditional household industry of handloom, which was exclusively a female business. But it was manifested during 1984-85 that most of women had undergone transition by giving up their traditional industry under the impact of modernisation. Women of Barmans especially younger generation were more allured by new fashions and dresses.

Table-4 exhibits that during 1961-1985 the percentage of women agricultural labourers has increased from 1.3 to 31.1 where as the percentage of women cultivators had declined to 48.5 from 55.8. This has been due to acute poverty and indebtedness resulting in conversion of cultivator families into agricultural labourers. The percentage of women in household industries has fallen from 41.9 to 14.13 during the said period. With regard to the category "other services" the percentage of women labourers has increased from .69 per cent to 3.8 per cent during the same period.

Let us compare the occupational pattern of the Scheduled tribe women with overall women population of the valley as per 1971 census.

The census report of 1971 clearly depicts the occupational shift of tribal women of Barak valley. Compared to general population, the Barman tribals in general and women in particular represented a megre percentage in activities like livestock, forestry and plantation.

Remarkably a significant percentage of tribal women labourers engaged in household industry compared to general population.

It is revealed from the table-5 that the percentage of cultivator woman (25.9) is much higher in tribal population than general population 9.6 per cent.

TABLE - 4

Occupational Pattern of the Barman, 1961 and 1985 (Rural Area)

Sl. No.	Category of workers	1961 No. of Barman workers M	F	T	1961 Percentage of total Barman workers. M	F	T	1984-85 No. of Barman workers M	F	T	1984-85 Percentage of total Barman workers M	F	T
1.	Cultivators.	2684	1448	4132	89.4	55.8	73.7	157	89	246	48.7	48.34	48.5
2.	Agricultural Labourers	174	35	209	5.8	1.3	3.7	78	59	137	24.2	32.1	27.02
3.	Livestock, Forestry, Plantation Planation. Mining and Quarrying.	2	1	3	.07	.04	.5	29	3	32	8.98	1.63	6.31
4.	Household industries	10	1994	1104	.33	41.9	19.7	-	26	26	-	14.13	5.1
5.	In Manufacturing Other than household industries	2	-	2	.07	-	.03	2	-	2	.02	-	.39
6.	Construction	3	13	16	.1	.5	.28	-	-	-	-	-	-
7.	Trade & Commerce	4	-	4	-13	-	.07	-	-	-	-	-	-
8.	Transport, Communication & Storage.	-	-	-	-	-	-	2	-	2	.62	-	.39
9.	Other Services	122	18	140	4.07	.69	2.49	55	7	62	17.02	3.8	12.2
	Total	3001	2609	5610	100	100	100	323	184	507	100	100	100

Source : Census of India, 1961, vol III, Part V-As Scheduled Castes and Scheduled Tribes. E.H. Pakyatein, I.A.S. page 178-79.

TABLE - 5

Occupation Pattern of the Scheduled Tribes & General Population in 1971.

Sl. No.	*Category of workers*	*Scheduled Tribe*			*General Population*		
		Percen-tage to total male workers	*Percen-tage to total female workers*	*Percen-tage to total workers*	*Percen-tage to total male workers*	*Percen-tage to total female workers*	*Percen-tage to total workers*
1.	Cultivator	71.1	25.93	66.95	50.06	9.6	46.7
2.	Agricultural Labourers	10.9	17.01	11.52	20.46	13.96	19.9
3.	Livestock, Forestry and plantation	2.8	0.83	2.6	8.1	58.77	12.3
4.	Mining and Quarrying	-	-	-	0.02	-	0.02
5.	Household industries	1.8	48.13	6.32	1.6	3.71	1.61
6.	Other than Household industries	0.11	0.62	0.16	2.04	1.7	2.01
7.	Construction	2.9	-	0.26	1.22	0.17	1.13
8.	Trade and Commerce	6.17	-	5.57	5.19	0.19	4.85
9.	Transportation, communication & storage	0.47	0.27	0.45	2.59	0.37	2.41
10.	Other services	6.03	7.36	6.15	8.88	10.76	9.04
	Total	100	100	100	100	100	100

Work Participation Rates

The work participation rate of the scheduled tribe population is higher than that of the general population in the Barak Valley in both

1961 and 1971 (Table 6). The 1961 data reveal that the female participation rate in case of Scheduled tribe of the Barak Valley is about three times higher than that of the general population. Regarding the participation of females in South Asian Countries, Gunner Myrdal[3] wrote: "India appears to be in an intermediate position with respect to the work performance of women, total abstentionism by higher caste women being accompanied by almost complete female participation among the low caste". This comment seems to be inapplicable if we taken in to account the participation rate of the females in 1971. The female participation rate of the scheduled tribe of Barak valley fall drastically to 6.65 in 1971 from 39.25 in 1961. The female participation rate for scheduled tribe in Barak Valley in 1971 differs very little with that of overall population. This is because of the difference in the concept of different category of workers in both Censuses. Many females who carried on with weaving purely for home consumption were included in the category of workers in 1961, whereas they were left out in 1971. Another striking feature is that participation rate for the scheduled tribe male was lower than that of the overall population in 1961 but in 1971 it became higher than that of the general population.

TABLE - 6

Participation Rates among Scheduled Tribes and General Population in 1961 and in 1971 in the Barak Valley

Census Year	Scheduled Tribe worker			Participation rate of Scheduled Tribe			Participation rate of General population		
	Male	Female	Total	Male	Female	Total	Male	Female	Total
1961	3251	2680	5931	44.85	39.25	42.13	53.7	13.8	34.7
1971	3170	125	3295	55.88	6.56	32.19	50.4	5.2	28.7

Source : i) Statistical Hand Book Assam, 1971, Directorate of Economic and Stitistics, Govt. of Assam, p. 13.

ii) Statistical Abstract Assam, 1961, Directorate of Economics and Statistics, Govt. of Assam, p. 10.

iii) Census of India, 1971 India Series I Paper I of 1975 Scheduled Castes and Scheduled Tribes, R.B. Chari. The Participation Rate is calculated by the author with the help of available date in the above Census Reports.

Status of Education Among Women

It is pertinent to focus light on education of women in Barak valley. It is heartening to note that as per 1971 census the tribal literacy rate is 30.5 percent which stands at a par with general population (30.6%). The women literacy rate for tribal is 22.4 per cent which is higher than that of general women literacy (19.9%) as per 1971 census. The general women litcracy in all India context is 18.7 per cent where as tribal women literacy is as low as 4.9 per cent. But surprisingly the sample survey conducted by the author in 1984-85 reveals that 34.5 per cent of women in Barak valley were literate.

Of course, though in terms of female literacy rate we behold an encouraging percentage but the level of educational achievement has been dismal. In regard to the level of educational attainment, most of the literate persons did not pass their primary level examination. As per 1961 census, out of 13114 Barmans 4449 were literate ; but only 862 persons had educational attainment with 822 having cross primary or junior basis level and 40 securing matriculation level or above.

However, there has emerged a remarkable change in the attainment of educational level within these 24 years. The data relating to this and procured from the sample survey under taken by the author in 1985 are presented in Table-7. Thus, it is seen that only 37.86 per cent for the total male population and 23.73 per cent of the female had an educational level ranging from the primary to the post-graduate standard. But, in regard to the enrollment at higher stages, they are quite behind the general population, especially the higher caste population among the Hindus.

Avialability of Schoolling Facilities

Availabililty of schooling facilities is one of the most important factors responsible for improving the status of education. Our investigation reveals that all the sample villages have schooling facilities at the primary level mostly within walking distances. The schooling facilities up to M.E. level of education within 3 kms. is found to be existing in about 89 per cent of the villages. But High School facilities are not available within the walking distance in most of the villages.

TABLE - 7

Educational level of the Barmans (1985)

Educational level	Male	Female	Percentage of Male to total male of population	Percentage of Females to the total female population
Primary to Class VII	98	62	16.2	11.58
Class VIII to Non-Matriculate	70	45	11.58	8.41
Matriculate/HSLC	45	19	7.45	3.55
P.U.H.S.S.L.C.	8	1	1.32	.19
Graduate	4	X	.66	X
Post-graduate	X	X	X	X
Matric and Technically educated	2	X	.33	X
Non-matric Technically educated	1	X	.16	X
Doctor	1	X	.16	X
Total Sample population	604	535	37.86	23.73

Source : Sample survey by the author.

Among the sample forest villages, to cite some examples the students of Lakhinagar have to trek a distance of 8 Kms. and these of Bilaipur and of Dhanipur have walk for 12 Kms. and 6 Kms. respectively to avail the educational facilities of high school standard. These forest villages are very backward from the point of view of education, health and communication. Besides these villages, the student of some other villages also have to walk for 5 Kms. to 20 Kms. on foot. As most of the villages are situated in the interior areas the students leave their education after LP/ME level. This is one of the causes of low level of educational attainment and high drop-out rates.

Though it is beyond the scope of present work to analyse vividly the various problems of educational system, yet a brief reference to this will be relevant here. Educationability depends on social as well as economic factors. Previously most of the parents disliked female education. They did not send their girls to the schools. Those who sent them to schools, mostly made them stop half way to the lower primary level itself. But the attitude of the majority of parents has undergone a radical change by the time. They have now been sending their female wards to schools. But most of the girl students, owing to long distance, have to close their educational pursuits after primary or M.E. level.

Secondly, the number of non-school going children was very large in the pre-independence period. In the mean time, however, a trend reversal is in sight. The number of drop-outs though large still, has fallen. Among the various causes of drop-outs, mention may be made of the presence of many single-teacher schools,[5] untrained and unqualified teachers.[6]

The preceeding paragraphs brought to light that there has been an insignificant change in the occupational pattern of the Barman women. They mostly depend on primary sector for their livelihood.

In the realm of education, their literacy percentage is more or less at par with general population of the Barak valley. Because of factors mentioned earlier, the level of educational attainment is abysmally low though literacy percentage is impressive.

Notes and References

1. Gait, Edward : 1926 - A History of Assam, 2nd edition, Reprint 1981, L.B.S. Publications, Panbazar, page-5.

2. At the time of Survey there were two districts in the Barak valley.

3. Myrdal, Gunner : 1968 Asian Drama, Vol. II, page 1073.

4. Census of India 1961, Series 3, Part VA, Scheduled Castes and Scheduled Tribes, p. 302 and 289.

5. The single teacher school remains closed when the teacher remains absent. In the I.T.D.P. area out of 64 primary schools, 38 schools are single teacher ones. (*Source* : Deputy Inspector of Schools, Silchar.)

   The problems of single-teacher school are discussed in the Book : N.C.E.R.T. 1972 : An Experiment in Teaching in Single - Teacher Schools in Rural Areas.

6. Regarding quality and role of teacher : Choudhury, R.K. : The New Education Policy and its missing links (iii) News Star, 25th June 1986 and Radhakrishna, S : True Knowledge, page 37.

   The teacher-pupil area, the total number of trained and untrained teachers were 39 and 53 respectively as 30.9.84
   (*Source* : D.I. of Schools, Silchar)

7. The teacher-pupil ratio of the primary schools of the I.T.D.P. area is 1:32 as against 1:43 in the Silchar Sub-division as a whole as on 30.9.84.
   (*Source* : D.I. of Schools, Silchar)

8. Without these a psychological grounding for the attraction of the students cannot be made.

7

A Case Study of Women Potters in Dakshina Kannada District of Karnataka

*A.V. Yadappanavar**

Introduction

Traditional rural industries of India have undergone a sea-change. The proportion of rural artisans fell from 18 per cent in 1901 to seven per cent in 1979. The decrease appears to have been caused by the uneconomic returns from the traditional occupation of artisans.

The mid-plan appraisal of Seventh Five Year Plan indicated that women beneficiaries of the IRDP were less than five per cent of the total. A special programme with an experimental approach, called Development of Women and Children in Rural Areas (DWCRA), was, therefore, introduced as a sub-scheme of IRDP in the second half of the Sixth Plan in 50 selected districts on pilot basis. The scheme was in operation in 290 districts during 1992-93, where rural women's poverty was believed to be most acute. DWCRA was designed to reach a package of development assistance to groups of poor women, with the objectives of improving their economic, health, educational and social status.

In Karnataka DWCRA is being implemented for several years in eight districts i.e., Bijapur, Mysore, Gulbarga, Chickmagalur, Kodagu, Dharwad, Raichur and Dakshina Kannada. It has recently been extended to three more districts i.e., Kolar, Bellary and Shimoga.

* Research Associate in NIRD, Hyderabad.

WCRA in Dakshina Kannada*

Dakshina Kannada is the first district in the country to assist all the 50 informal groups. The lead bank manager of the district Syndicate Bank stated that this was mainly because the Dakshina Kannada Zilla Parishad had provided subsidy to the beneficiaries. The subsidy utilisation was to the tune Rs. 8.23 lakhs and the loan amount provided by the lead bank too was Rs. 8.23 lakhs during the year 1990-1991.

In Dakshina Kannada, 200 groups were formed between 1988-89 and March, 1991. Besides, Dakshina Kannada has been selected along with Raichur as pilot project district. Under the pilot project scheme informal groups and unregistered groups are financed by the Syndicate bank, which is the lead bank of the district. The salient features of pilot project under informal groups are the minimum number of members will be five. Each such group will be entitled to revolving fund on prorata basis at Rs. 1,000/- per member subject to ceiling of Rs. 15,000/- per group. The group will also be entitled to subsidy at 50 per cent subject to the monetary ceiling prescribed under IRDP guidelines.

The activities of the DWCRA groups are both of the traditional and non-traditional types. The number of members in each group varies between 5 and 17. It was observed during the study that the informal groups under the pilot project scheme as distinct from the general project took up non-traditional activities mainly, such as sericulture, gem-cutting, polishing marble-stones, stone querrying etc.

Dakshina Kannada holds the distinction of pioneering under the roofing tile industry in the country. Over 100 units produce a wide range of clay products. The phenomenal growth of the clay industry is mainly due to the abundant availability of excellent clay on the river beds.

The number of women groups engaged in mineral based activities is hardly six per cent in the district.

Rural astisans highly skilled in pottery are, compelled to give up their traditional craft and go in search of other jobs for their

* Govt. of Karnataka, Socio-Economic Survey of Dakshina Kannada, 1988-89 (Report), Mangalore District Statistics Office, 1990.

livelihood. In 1901, there were three million rural potters in India and this number came down to 1.2 million in 1971. This represents a 60 per cent decline in number.

There are two types of clay potteries, viz., red and blue. Red clay pottery still has an important place in rural households as providing utensils for cooking, eating and drinking purposes. A concentration of potters is still find a place in number of villages. A large section of poor peasants and agricultural labourers in rural areas still patronise the village potter. Water containers made of red clay are still considered ideal storing water, due to their property of cooling water in the summer. Similarly garden pots, eating and drinking pots for animals and toys and from red clay are generally in demand. This explains the survival of potters in rural areas. People prefer red clay pottery as it is comparatively cheap and the raw materials needed for it are easily available.

An in-depth analysis of the poverty alleviation programmes clearly shows that the only effective way lies in providing employment opportunities in the traditional village industry sector.

Objectives of the Study

The objectives of the present study are to examine the relative impact of 'DWCRA' on female beneficiaries in the Kulai village of the Dakshina Kannada district and to examine the problems faced by them in running their self-employment ventures.

Methodology

Study Area and Sample

It was decided to conduct this study that was known to have had a moderate performance record in regard to DWCRA, and the state of Karnataka was accordingly selected. Discussions were held with the officials of the state government, so as to assess the performance of the unit chosen. Based on this, Dakshina Kannada district was selected for study, and specifically the Kulai village was chosen. It was proposed to cover only six respondents, since the emphasis was on intensive rather than extensive coverage of samples. With this end in view, a unit of women potters set up in October, 1990 was taken up for study.

Method

Collection of primary data covered the personal status and personal, socio-economic background of the respondents. Some of the variables are personal-social background - the family status, occupational status, awareness of official machinery, satisfaction level of social services, attitude to infrastructural support of the chosen occupation.

A structured interview scheduled was used to collect the information from the samples, who were the beneficiaries of the DWCRA programme. Discussion was held with govt. officials in order to understand the efforts made by them to promote the development of women. Data were collected during August, 1992.

Socio-Economic Profile of Beneficiaries

Four of the samples were in the age group of 35 and above, five were married and belonged to nuclear families. Five of them had studied upto primary level and all had an income upto Rs. 11,000/- per annum. All had contact with the Gram Sevika and the Assistant Project Officer.

They kept contact with the officials concerned so as to keep themselves informed of the various aspects of their scheme. Use of spare time meaningfully and providing financial support to the family were the major reasons for samples to become members of the DWCRA scheme.

*Raw Materials and Manufacturing Process**

The chief raw material required for the scheme is fine clay. Clay is sometimes kneaded with horsedung or sand before it is used. Kneaded clay is placed on the potter's wheel. Making of earthen vassels depends more on the skill of hand than on the equipment. The vessels are first sun-dried and then carried in baskets to the furnace for baking. The baked vessels are then ready for sale.

During the study, it was observed that houses of the beneficiaries was used as working shed for carrying on the activity and also for stocking raw materials.

* Technical Consultancy Services Organisation of Karnataka (1991), Five Year Perspective Plan Development of Tiny Industries in 'DWCRA' districts of Dakshin Kannada.

During the field visit of the study team, the beneficiaries said that clay used to be brought from Polali at a cost of Rs. 1,000/- per load and out of which this vessels worth about Rs. 4,000 - 5,000 could be made. Fine sand which is mixed with clay is brought in a tempo and costs them Rs. 60/- per load.

Each beneficiary has one potter's wheel. The products made include hanging pots, cooking vessels, pots for plants, plates etc. About 600 pots of different varieties are made every month. The beneficiaries carried them in baskets to places such as Kodikal and Ashoknagar, which were situated within a radius of about 5 to 20 kms. The price of the pots varied from Rs. three to ten. The beneficiaries were able to earn Rs. 614/- per month.

Marketing

The majority of them were satisfied with the marketing facility. Either a shop was opened or they used to go to a weekly market or local markets. They seem to estimate the demand based on their observation of the market trends. During festivals and marriage seasons, the sales increased significantly. During the slack season, for want of demand and for the risk involved in storing raw materials, the work used to be stopped. Thus, there was seasonal fluctuation in the sales volume. In the rainy season, the potters are forced to work on daily wage basis as casual agricultural labourers.

Skill and Technology

Technology is crucial for productivity and for bringing about a positive change in the economic and social profile of rural women potters. But the present policy formulation and implementation systems have been less than sensitive to the technological requirements of these people. This has to undergo a change. If this is to happen, the rural potters must strengthen their ability to give an organised expression of their needs. This may even mean considerable social change through educational programmes. Yet, until this happens, whatever is attempted in terms of technological improvement may not be sufficient to better the lot of these people. The success of a pottery unit needs an infrastructural support coupled with financial support for the effective functioning. The details of the cost analysis is presented below :

Fixed Investment

1. (a) Building : Own premises
   (b) Power : For lighting purpose only
   (c) Water : For process and human consumption.

2. Working capital requirement :

(a) Clay	Rs. 1,000
(b) Fuel & Transportation	Rs. 500
Total	Rs. 1,500/-

3. Cost of project :

(a) Building :	Own premises
(b) Furnace	Rs. 3,000
(c) Machinery & equipment	Rs. 500
d) Working capital p.m.	Rs. 1,500
Total	Rs. 5,000

4. Means of finance

(a) Loan amount	Rs. 2,500
(b) Subsidy amount	Rs. 2,500

5. Expected expenditure per month :

(a) Working capital	Rs. 1,500
(b) Interest @ 10% pm	Rs. 21
(c) Depreciation @ 95% pm	Rs. 40
Total	Rs. 1,561

6. Financial Analysis :

a) Sale of 200 big pots for Rs. 8 each	Rs. 1,600
b) Sale of 200 small pots for Rs. 2.50	Rs. 500
c) Sale of 50 plates for Rs. 1.50 each	Rs. 75
Total	Rs. 2,175
Profit	Rs. 614

Satisfaction with Facilities and Service

The majority of respondents felt that cooperation from district level officials and banks were adequate.

Problems Related to Marketing

The beneficiaries' level of knowledge of marketing was very poor and the crucial functions of marketing were not known to them. Consequently, they were not able to plan their production to match the needs of the market and to obtain reasonable prices for their products. Potters at the moment earn a very small income as their products scarcely find any large potential market except for the local villagers' demand for them. The limitedness of the market is directly related to the limited product range and small earnings. It was revealed that most of the potters were selling their products in their own villages and the nearby towns. Since, these beneficiaries have no knowledge of market not much profits could be generated. The products were sold at rock-bottom prices. As their products were limited to pots, household and kitchen wares, these products could not survivie due to competition from aluminium, steel and plastic products of urban areas.

They should resort to diversified product, which require the same clay and skill they can be assured of better earnings. Garden-pots, sheetaks, claypipes, floorings and fancy tiles, smokeless chulhas, clarings for biogas plants etc., are better paying articles as compared to the traditional items like pots, and pans.

In order to have a wider market they have to sell their products in places of religious importance, like Udupi, Dharmasthala, Mangalore etc.

Recommendations

1. It is recommended that the state Handicraft Board need to be established at every district headquarters. These regional centres will procure the products from these units and market them.

2. For marketing the products manufactured by DWCRA groups, tie up within the DWCRA groups, such as pottery and with various Govt. departments District Supply and marketing society, DICs, private entrepreneurs, active women multipurpose cooperative societies, Janata Bazars can be taken into consideration. Mandal and Zilla Parishads initiative in this matter will be helpful.

3. A.P.O. needs to arrange with the Khadi and Village Industries Board to give training to members of this unit for six months in the skills of making terracotta items like flower pots, flower vases, pen stands, candle stands, lamp shades, wall plates idols etc. Not only traditional items but creative designs and innovative terracotta items, which have an appeal for the urban consumers as well. They should be taught the scientific way of kneading the clay. The method of using the hand to shape the artifacts and making of moulds. As an improvement over the traditional potters wheel the more efficient Khanapur potters's wheel needs to be introduced there and should be given training in handling it. Zilla Parishad should take the responsibility of helping them to market novel Terracotta items.

4. Presently only the leadbank, syndicate bank finances the informal DWCRA groups under pilot project. With the likelihood of more informal groups getting formed in future years, the loan assistance to such groups can be extended by other nationalised banks in the district.

8

Problems of Rural Women Workers in Readymade Garments : Andhra Pradesh and Karnataka

*Dr. A. Mohiuddin & Dr. Vikram Singh**

Summary

Objectives and Methodology

Garment making is one of the earliest professions in which women have been engaged to supplement their income. This scheme is bassed on the fact that tailoring is still considered as a most suited, traditional and handy income generation activity for women in rural areas and a large number of sewing machines continue to be provided to women under this scheme.

The project to study "problems of Rural Women Workers engaged in Readymade Garments in the States of Andhra Pradesh and Karnataka", was sponsored by the Department of Women and Child Development, Ministry of Human Resource Development, Government of India. The present research was organised in the States of Andhra Pradesh and Karnataka with the following objectives :

1. To study the socio-economic profile of rural women workers engaged in tailoring and readymade garment activities.

2. To ascertain their working conditions, job opportunities, income patterns, wages, nature of work.

* Dr. A. Mohiuddin and Dr. Vikram Singh belong to faculty positions in NIRD, Hyderabad. Dr. Mohiuddin is the Director (Women Studies) NIRD.

3. To assess raw material requirements.

4. To observe marketing patterns.

5. To gather awareness of protective

6. To gauge the impact of economic activity on their social status.

Four hundred respondents, 200 each from Andhra Pradesh and Karnataka states were selected. Semi-structured interview schedules and case study method and observations were the mode of date collection. Ten representative case studies were also prepared, in order to have an indepth understanding of the profile of rural women working in the unorganised sector of garment making.

Workers Profile

Some of the important characteristics of the garment workers are discussed below :

Age

Over half the number of total women garment makers were in the younger age group of 15-24 years, whereas only five respondents, of whom four from Karnataka alone, were of more than 45 years. Across the states, the number of women in each age group were almost equal. Skill development and training may be focussed among younger age groups (15-30 years) (Table-1.)

Marital Status

Almost two thirds of the total respondents were married women which was followed by unmarried. The number of unmarried women was noticeably more from Andhra Pradesh than from Karnataka. In other categories, there were no significant differences noticed between the two states. The number of widowed and divorced women was considerably low in the study sample.

Religion

Though the major part of the sample consisted of Hindus, there were respondents from Christians and Muslim communities also. The sample was drawn from Scheduled Caste, Scheduled Tribe, Backward Caste and Forward Class. The distribution of Scheduled Tribes and Christian respondents were unequal in the three districts of the study.

Educational Level

An analysis of the educational level of the respondents revealed that most of the women from Scheduled Caste and Scheduled Tribe were illiterates. The majority of the respondents had studied upto primary level and there were only five graduate respondents in the sample.

Occupational Multiplicity : Need to Earn

As far as occupational multiplicity is concerned, it was found that the majority of women engaged themselves in tailoring as their main occupation, in order to earn their livelihood or to supplement their family income. The need to earn was the principal motivation.

As regards the categorisation of sample respondents, the inter-state differences in the four categories were evident. The categories consisted of :

1. Purely readymade garment makers ;
2. Mainly readymade garment makers and occasional tailors ;
3. Purely tailors ; and
4. Mainly tailors and occasional readymade garment makers.

Almost 75 per cent of the sample was constituted by tailors. The majority of these women were homebased. Only a small percentage of the respondents were predominantly involved in readymade garment production.

It was observed that the work in garment making was not available to all the women regularly and therefore, they had no option but to take up some other income generating activity. Hence, during slack seasons, most of the women were doing agriculture labour and a few of them were engaged in beedi making and match box making as their secondary occupation.

Income and Expenditure Patterns

An analysis of respondents' income from garment making indicated that women from Andhra Pradesh earned substantially higher amount than their counterparts from Karnataka. It was noticed that the average income of the readymade garment workers was slightly more than the tailors. This difference was attributed to the availability of regular work in readymade garment production.

The income received from garment making was mainly used for household purposes. In most of the cases, the women looked at their contribution as marginal in terms of economic help to the family. 25 per cent of the respondents perceived their contribution as crucial because their earnings were the chief source of household income. As regards to the gross annual income, it was noticed that the number of respondents in the income group of Rs. 7500/- and above were distinctly more in Karnataka than Andhra Pradesh. The respondents having the gross annual income of Rs. 7500/- and above were more in Andhra Pradesh. It is important to note that a substantial part of the sample is constituted by the destitutes women. Their proportion in both the states are varying. (Table-2)

Working Conditions

A large number of home-based women from both the states found the working conditions congenial and adequate in their houses. Most of these women would work only during the day time when there was adequate light and ventilation.

The majority of women, who were making readymade garments at home, had to collect the raw material and deliver the stitched clothes 'on their own'. The agents would not come to their houses. In case of tailors, the customers would deliver and collect the finished goods themselves. The predominant reason. For the women working at home was household responsibilities.

There were a few women Andhra Pradesh, who mentioned that their family members were opposed to the idea of women working outside the home, or that their religion did not permit them working outside. For another few women, the units or work places were far from their homes, as a result of which they were forced to be homebased. Child care responsibilities were also one of the reasons for being homebased. Most of the homebased workers mentioned that they would not mind working outside the home, if (i) regularity in employment in assured (ii) work place is in close proximity to the residence (iii) suitable child care facilities at the work place are available and (iv) flexible working hours are allowed.

The working conditions and the other facilities were stated to be satisfactory only for those who were working with units/centres established under any Government, scheme. Whereas, for those who are working in the unorganised sector, the working conditions were voiced as 'unsatisfactory'.

Piece-rate was the mode of remuneration for all the respondents, barring a negligible number or women from Andhra Pradesh, who received some portion of remuneration in kind, usually food grains in unorganised sector.

Problems

The problems in terms of receiving the payment ranged from delay in payment to not receiving the entire amount. The majority of them did not have any problem in getting raw material. Of the rest, some complained about the transport of raw material, whereas others mentioned that shop keepers did not give the material on credit, which resulted in their losing customers.

Other problems cited by most of the respondents were (i) payment in irregular installments (ii) low/poor quality of raw material (iii) employer's/customers' bad treatment (iv) low demand for the trade (Table 3).

As far as rates were concerned, they ranged from 50 paise to Rs. 6/- based upon the expertise of the tailor, size of the dress, design and type of raw material used. There were to distinct inter-state differences in the rates. In general, the rates were considered very low in comparison to commercial tailors, especially for those engaged in readymade garment production. However, women had no option but to accept these rates, for fear of losing the customers.

By and large, the respondents both from Andhra Pradesh and Karnataka felt that the males in general, were getting higher rates for the same kind of work. Male tailors were believed to be more professional and better trained by their employers as compared to their female counterparts. A considerable number of women attributed their predicament to their being homebased, which resulted in their having no bargaining power and thereby no option but to accept the existing rates. Most of these women did not raise objections to the existing rates due to the fear of losing their customers.

Training

As regards training, skills, the majority of the women had received training, formal or informal, in garment making. The source of formal training was by and large, government schemes such as TRYSEM and DWCRA. During the training women were paid stipend/wages ranging from Rs. 50/- to Rs. 150/- per month. The other sources of training were voluntary agencies and private tailors. The informal training was imparted to the respondents either by relatives or by neighbours/friends, or in their own families, as garment making was their family occupation. Training was low-cost and time-bound. This leads us to suggest that quality attainment in terms of training be considered as an important criteria, rather than the time factor. Further attempts are due to make women into trained 'Professionals' rather than as 'Casual Workers'. (Table - 4 & 5).

It is important to note that the majority of the women from Andhra Pradesh were trained under Govt. schemes while in Karnataka, more than half of the women were trained by voluntary agencies and private tailors. All trained respondents underwent a course for at least two months. The majority of these women were satisfied with the duration and nature of training. They felt that it was sufficient for acquiring the skills they were interested in. However, it was desired by many, that new skills also should be imparted to enhance the job opportunities, hence diversification of skills and alternatives in job markets are suggested.

As regards the type of trainers, the majority of the women were trained by private tailors and Govt. teachers. The trainers were predominantly female in both the states. There were very few women trained by professional tailors or by family members.

As far as areas of training are concerned, it was desired that more and more gent's garments and the latest designs should be included in the syllabus because of increased demand and higher remuneration. As regards quality of teaching, few of them expressed discontentment. They suggested better trained and experienced teachers and master craftsmen/women, as a solution. By and large, the women were benefitted from training, not only in terms of skill, but also in enhancing their income from garment making. It was desired that more and more employment opportunities should be made available to all the trained women.

Hours of Work

It was noticed that on an average, the working hours for garment making were about 4 hours per day. Whereas for household chores women devoted 7 hours a day. No significant differences were noticed on this variable between the two study states.

Less working hours could be attributed to the non-availability of the sufficient work in garment making.

Help Received

As regards the household chores, in both the states, it was noticed that most of the women performed all the household work on their own, except a few who were assisted by their mothers-in-law/mothers and daughters. Only 14 women reported the help given by husband or any other male member of the family. However, help received by women workers did not increase the income of the women due to dearth of customers.

A large number of women tailors had their own sewing machines. Among those who did not own the machines, were those either working in readymade garment production units or who took on rent basis or borrowed from relatives/friends etc. A few women were financed by banks/voluntary agencies for purchase of sewing machines.

The majority of the tailors did not use iron boxes. As regards maintenance of their equipment, the majority of homebased and readymade garment workers handled minor repairs on their own, but got the major repairs done by mechanics. For all these women, a major breakdown meant the loss of work and thereby loss of income.

Customers/Clients

The majority of the respondents gave village leaders 'households as their chief customers. Wholesale dealers and agents within rural areas constituted the customers of those women who were engaged in readymade garments, mostly from Andhra Pradesh. In unorganised sector agents sold the products only in rural areas, due to poor quality of finished products. In case of government establishments, it was observed that the products were supplied to Govt. hostels, hospitals and schools. The feasibility of starting co-operative marketing centres for readymade garment workers under Govt. schemes may be experimented on priority.

Barring very few women who got the cloth and other raw materials from agents, the majority of the respondents had to buy it from the retailers. Cash payment was the most common mode of these transactions.

Awareness in Functioning of Units/Centres

As regards mode of functioning of the Units/Centres/Schemes, an overwhelming percentage of readymade garment makers did not know the source of orders, their employers/agents got, nor where these garments were sold or distributed. They further mentioned, that it was none of their concern to get the products publicised.

As far as their involvement in decision making in the unit/ establishment affairs is concerned, the majority of the women reported 'no involvement'. Thus accepting themselves as 'Unseen' and 'Un-noticed' labour.

Aptitude and Performance

As far as aptitude for garment making was concerned, not much difference was noticed between men's and women's performances provided both were given a similar type of training. However, the performance was attributed to their interest, patience and neatness in work. This profession was linked with women because of its homebased income generating potential and also because of its gender appropriateness.

It was projected by the majority of women that garment making is a drudgery oriented profession, hence most of the men prefer to opt to other avocations open for them, whereas women have lack of alternatives outside the homes, hence they continued to accept it as a profession inspite of its drudgery.

Respondents attitude towards garment making for their children was also assessed. It was evident that the majority of the respondents did not consider it suitable for their sons. The reasons mentioned were 'Low demand for the trade' and 'no regular work'. However, for daughters the profession was viewed as good and an easy way to earn money.

Status and Decision Making

Though a major portion of income from garment making was used for the household purposes, most of the decisions regarding food, clothing, housing, purchase of equipment, schooling of sons and daughters were taken by husbands/fathers or the heads of the family without consulting the respondent. Women workers had a very little role to play in the decision making patterns of the family. Most of the women did not have liberty even to decide about the matters related to garment making such as purchase of equipments. Even after being the chief earner of the family, their status was not enhanced considerably. Of course, in the case of a few married women, their economic contribution was well recognised and as a result of it, they received good treatment from their husbands. The economic role of the women is still being shadowed by male oriented values and attitudes in rural areas. Women still accept their 'Secondary' position without questioning it. (Table-6).

Awareness of Facilities and Legislative Laws

The provision of leave, paid lunch break or compensation at the time of accidents, were not available to those who were engaged in the units of readymade garment production. It is important to note that all the women were piece rate workers and if they availed leave or could not attend the work due to some unavoidable reasons, they had to forego their remunerations. Their income largely depended on the amount of work they did. This is applicable for Government schemes as well.

By and large the women workers were not aware of the various legislations stipulated by the Govt. such as Equal Remuneration Act (1976), Maternity Benefits Act (1961) and Minimum Wages Act (1968).

In a few cases, it was observed that employer's design strategies by which women in the organised/unorganised sector do not become eligible for enjoying these facilities under such laws. Hence, it is recommended that Govt./women's organisations should have a check on such malpractices of the employers. Procedures for eligibility should also be streamlined and wide publicity may be given for proper enforcement of the same.

TABLE - 1

Distribution of Respondents by Age

State	*15-19*	*20-24*	*25-29*	*30-34*	*35-39*	*40-44*	*45-59*	*Total*
Andhra Pradesh	*72*	*46*	*38*	*33*	*6*	*4*	*1*	*200*
Cuddapah	(36.00)	(23.00)	(19.00)	(16.50)	(3.0)	(2.0)	(0.05)	(100.00)
Karnataka	*59*	*47*	*35*	*34*	*15*	*6*	*4*	*200*
	(29.50)	(23.50)	(17.50)	(17.00)	(7.5)	(3.00)	(2.00)	(100.00)
Biddar	38	29	12	16	3	1	1	100
Belgaum	21	18	23	18	12	5	3	100
Total	131	93	73	67	21	10	5	400
	(32.75)	(23.25)	(18.25)	(16.75)	(5.25)	(2.50)	(1.25)	(100.00)

TABLE - 2

Family Gross Annual Income

State	*Upto Rs. 3000*	*Rs. 3001 to Rs. 4500*	*Rs. 4501 to Rs. 6000*	*Rs. 6001 to Rs. 7500*	*Rs. 7501 to Rs. 9000*	*Rs. 9001 to Rs. 10500*	*Rs. 10500 and above*	*Total*
Andhra Pradesh	*38*	*39*	*41*	*29*	*7*	*11*	*35*	*200*
Cuddapah	(19.00)			(14.95)				(100.00)
Karnataka	*25*	*30*	*31*	*20*	*14*	*11*	*69*	*200*
	(12.50)	(15.00)	(15.50)	(10.00)	(7.00)	(10.50)	(34.50)	(100.00)
Biddar	11	17	13	7	7	9	36	100
Belgaum	14	13	18	13	7	2	33	100
Total	63	69	72	49	21	22	104	400
	(15.75)	(17.25)	(18.00)	(12.25)	(5.25)	(5.50)		(100.00)

TABLE - 3

General Problems in Garment Making

States	*Delay in payment*	*Payment in irregular instalments*	*Transport of raw material*	*Low quality of raw material*	*No credit / loan for purchase of material*	*Employers bad treatment*	*Low Demand*	*Total*
Andhra Pradesh	*55*	*9*	*17*	*2*	*10*	*13*	*21*	*127*
Cuddapah	(43.3)	(7.17)	(13.39)	(1.57)	(7.87)	(10.23)	(16.53)	(100.00)
Karnataka	*70*	*2*	*1*	*1*	*4*	*6*	*51*	*135*
	(51.85)	(1.5)	(0.74)	(0.74)	(2.96)	(4.44)	(37.7)	(100.00)
Biddar	44	-	1	-	2	3	42	92
Belgaum	26	2	-	1	2	3	9	43
Total	125	11	18	3	14	19	72	262
	(147.7)	(4.19)	(6.87)	(0.82)	(5.34)	(2.25)	(27.48)	(100.00)

TABLE - 4

Duration of Training

States	*Upto 1 month*	*2-4 months*	*5-7 months*	*8-10 months*	*11+ months*	*Total**
Andhra Pradesh	*1*	*8*	*42*	*64*	*53*	*168*
Cuddapah		(5.0)	(25.0)	(38.1)	(32.0)	(100.00)
Karnataka	*1*	*31*	*56*	*41*	*60*	*189*
		(16.0)	(30.0)	(22.0)	(32.0)	(100.0)
Biddar	1	16	27	14	33	91
Belgaum	-	15	29	27	27	98
Total	2	39	98	105	113	357
		(11.0)	(27.0)	(29.0)	(32.0)	(100.00)

* Does not include, not applicable (n = 11) and not answered (n = 32).

TABLE - 5

Benefits from Training

States	INCOME				SKILLS			
	Yes	*No*	*Not answered*	*Total*	*Yes*	*No*	*Not answered*	*Total*
(1)	(2)	(3)	(4)	(5)	(6)	(7)	(8)	(9)
Andhra Pradesh	*144*	*43*	*10*	*198*	*68*	*115*	*14*	*197*
Cuddapah	(72.8)	(21.7)	(5.0)	(100.0)	(34.5)	(75.8)	(7.1)	(100.0)
Karnataka	*158*	*30*	*9*	*197*	*127*	*60*	*9*	*196*
	(80.2)	(15.2)	(4.5)	(100.0)	(64.8)	(30.6)	(4.6)	(100.0)
Biddar	78	10	9	-	65	23	-	-
Belgaum	80	20	-	-	62	37	-	-
Total	302	73	19	395	195	175	23	393
	(76.5)	(18.5)	(4.8)	(100.0)	(49.6)	(44.5)	(5.9)	(100.00)

Contd.

TABLE - 5 (Cont'd)

Benefits from Training

States	EMPLOYMENT			Total	STATUS			Total
	Yes	No	Not answered		Yes	No	Not answered	
(1)	(10)	(11)	(12)	(13)	(14)	(15)	(16)	(17)
Andhra Pradesh	*57*	*127*	*13*	*197*	*25*	*155*	*16*	*196*
Cuddapah	(28.9)	(64.5)	(6.6)	(100.0)	(12.8)	(79.1)	(81.6)	(100.0)
Karnataka	*83*	*104*	*9*	*196*	*58*	*129*	*9*	*196*
	(42.3)	(53.1)	(4.5)	(100.0)	(29.6)	(65.8)	(4.6)	(100.0)
Biddar	42	46	9	-	25	65	9	-
Belgaum	41	58	-	-	35	64	-	-
Total	140	31	22	393	83	284	25	392
	(35.6)	(58.8)	(5.6)	(100.0)	(21.2)	(72.5)	(6.4)	(100.00)

TABLE - 6

Decision Making Pattern

State	Food (N = 400)				Clothing (N = 400)				Housing (N = 400)			
	Respon-dent	*Hus-band / Father*	*Both (1+2)*	*Other family members*	*Respon-dent*	*Hus-band / Father*	*Both (1+2)*	*Other family members*	*Respon-dent*	*Husb-band / Father*	*Both (1+2)*	*Other family members*
Andhra Pradesh	*40*	*97*	*36*	*27*	*32*	*103*	*34*	*31*	*32*	*103*	*34*	*31*
Cuddapah	(20.2)	(48.5)	(18.0)	(13.5)	(16.0)	(51.5)	(17.0)	(15.5)	(16.0)	(51.5)	(17.0)	(15.5)
Karnataka	*9*	*119*	*39*	*33*	*10*	*121*	*44*	*25*	*26*	*115*	*37*	*22*
	(4.5)	(59.5)	(19.5)	(16.5)	(5.0)	(60.5)	(22.0)	(12.5)	(13.0)	(57.5)	(18.5)	(11.0)
Biddar	2	71	12	15	2	72	13	13	3	73	11	13
Belgaum	7	48	27	18	8	49	31	12	23	42	26	9
	49	216	75	60	42	224	78	56	58	218	71	53
	(12.3)	(54.0)	(18.8)	(15.0)	(10.5)	(56.0)	(19.5)	(14.0)	(14.5)	(54.5)	(17.8)	(13.3)

Contd.

TABLE - 6 (Cont'd)

Decision Making Pattern

State	Purchase of Equipment (N = 00)				Education of sons (N = 261; 100.0)				Education of daughters (N = 261; 100.0)			
	Respon-dent	Hus-band / Father	Both (1+2)	Other family members	Respon-dent	Hus-band / Father	Both (1+2)	Other family members	Respon-dent	Hus-band / Father	Both (1+2)	Other family members
Andhra Pradesh	*61*	*77*	*31*	*31*	*18*	*61*	*30*	*8*	*17*	*60*	*28*	*8*
Cuddapah	(30.5)	(38.5)	(15.5)	(15.5)	(15.38)	(52.14)	(25.65)	(6.84)	(15.04)	(53.1)	(24.78)	(7.1)
Karnataka	*17*	*124*	*34*	*25*	*9*	*86*	*35*	*14*	*8*	*91*	*35*	*14*
	(8.5)	(62.0)	(17.0)	(12.5)	(6.25)	(59.72)	(24.31)	(9.72)	(5.41)	(61.49)	(23.65)	(9.46)
Biddar	5	56	13	13	2	41	12	7	2	45	12	7
Belgaum	12	68	21	12	7	45	23	7	6	46	23	7
	78	201	65	56	27	147	65	22	25	151	63	22
	(19.50)	(50.25)	(16.25)	(14.0)	(10.34)	(56.32)	(24.9)	(8.43)	(9.58)	(57.85)	(24.14)	(8.43)

Note :- The question regarding the schooling of sons /daughters was applicable only to 261 respondents who had children.

9

Women Labour in Construction Sector : A Study in Orissa

*Dr. S.N. Tripathy**

The present paper is an attempt to examine the Socio-economic profile of women construction labourers in Orissa along with an analysis of construction sector.

Construction, one of the oldest organised activities of human societies, has been employing a large segment of rural people much before the industrial development. As a result, the pre-industrial societies advanced labour intensive technique of construction, and established mode of integrating construction activity with the socio-economic structure of the society. The massive architectural monuments scattered all over the country provide the testimony regarding advanced state of techniques of construction in pre-industrial India.

During the industrialization phase, with the growth of urban metropolis, construction activities move to the cities. With the planned economic development adopted during five year plans, construction activities especially, in the form of socio-overhead capital (SOC) like road, bridge, building, river dams, railway construction etc. developed by leaps and bounds.

General Features of Construction Activities

The construction industry unorganised and not developed at a par with modern industrial sector. This sector has remained labour intensive production with low level of mechanization.

* Lecturer in Economics, Aska Science College.

Most of the feature of the organisation of this industry as well as the work relations are inherited for centuries from a pre-industrial society.

The modern construction sector in public as well as in private enterprises has been the ramification of colonial era. However, some of the basic ingredients has remained more or less same. For instance :

(i) The mason's status as artisans has remained intact even today.

(ii) The head mason or the maistry is a sub-contractor as well as heads a team of construction workers involved in a particular task.

(iii) The Maistry usually works with a team of workers of his choice and moves from site to site with more or less the same team.

(iv) The maistry is often, especially in small construction sites, free to choose the way he works; the order in which the work is to be completed etc.

(v) All the jobs are undertaken on a piece-rate basis. A maistry is contracted to complete a piece of work for a certain fixed payment.

(vi) The Caste system is still the institution within which apprentices are trained to become skilled workers, carpenters, masons etc, especially in villages and small towns;

(vii) Even in the formal industrial sector, the contractors in major construction sites, both private and public, are mere financiers with no understanding of the production process and labour management. They are considered as the 'implementor' of a plan by the main employer. The Production in construction sector has been carried out based on subcontract.

The Low Level of Mechanization

The levels of mechanization in the construction industry in India has remained low. Wherever some mechanization has taken place, it has been only marginal. Besides, the cheap supply of labour, a major cause of this low level of mechanization. Mechanization therefore, may not make immediate economic factor. Whatever the reasons, the fact of a low level of mechanization with the retention of labour intensive processes, makes it even more difficult to integrate the construction industry.

Organising Labourers and Inherent Problems

"The unorganised nature of the construction labour is directly linked to the process of production involved in this industry. In construction, unlike any other type of production, the product of labour remains stationary while the labour moves from site to site, from one employer to another. This is in contrast to any other type of production where the product of labour moves, while the labour force remain stationary under the same employer. Also, the different stages of construction are undertaken according to piece-rate by different maistrys and they engage different groups of labourers. Work is organised into masonary, carpentary, earthwork, concerting, curing, plumbing, painting and electrical work. Each group of workers is required for work at different times depending on the stage of construction . The concreting work for example would require the labour of a group of labourers for a single day after which the mason and his group moves to another site in search of construction work. The group moves from one site to another. The burden of finding employment for the group falls squarely on the maistry. These peculiarities in the nature of construction work are some of the causes for the unstable relationship between employer and employee, the insecurity of employment, difficulty in enforcing the existing labour laws and regulations related to this industry and the problems encountered while organizing the labour force."

"In big construction sites however, the opportunities for continuity of work, both for maistrys and all categories of labourers exist for longer duration. As a result, in big construction sites, it is possible to maintain records and ensure proper working conditions for its labourers. In reality, this does not take place. As these big construction sites are in a position to ensure continious employment for its workers and maistry's, they use this as a weapon to manoeuvre and exploit the employees. Thus, the oppurtunity for continious employment and the insecurity of work go hand in hand in big construction sites. Moreover, the system of subcontract is a deliberate choice of the formal industrial sector to deny recognition and responsibility towards the labour force."

Thus various factors peculiar to this industry namely high mobility of labour, changing employer-employee relationships and the 'forced labour' type of situations (prevailing in bigger construction sites), pose peculiar problems while attempting to organize the construction labour force. So long as the construction labourers are not unorganized and labour unions are not established it is not possible to change the scenario.

Data on Construction Labour

Reliable data on the number of workers employed in the construction industry are difficult to find out. According to the census data, the growth of the labour force on construction industry indicates a sharp rise from 1871 to 1901. The Twentieth century census data however indicate fluctuations during the first half of the century and increase in their numbers from 1951 onwards.

Table- 1 depicts the percentage distribution of main workers by industrial categories during 1981 to 1991 census.

TABLE - 1

Percentage Distribution of Main Workers by Industrial Categories.

	Industrail Category	*1981*		*1991*	
		Female	*Male*	*Female*	*Male*
1	2	3	4	5	6
(i)	Cultivators	33.09	43.71	34.22	39.63
(ii)	Agricultural labourers	46.34	19.57	44.93	21.05
(iii)	Livestock, Forestry, Fishing, Plantation and allied activities	1.83	2.37	1.60	1.94
(iv)	Priming and quarrying	0.35	0.63	0.34	0.70
	PRIMARY	81.61	66.28	81.09	63.38

(Contd.)

TABLE - 1 (contd.)

1	2	3	4	5	6
v. (a)	Manufacturing and processing, servicing and repair in House-hold industries.	4.57	3.18	3.53	2.09
(b)	Manufacturing and processing, servicing and repair in other than Household Industries	3.6	8.91	3.88	8.89
vi.	Constructions	0.87	1.87	0.66	2.32
	SECONDARY	9.04	13.96	8.07	13.30
vii	Trade and commerce	2.04	7.41	2.26	8.98
viii	Transport, storage & communication	0.37	3.36	0.32	3.54
ix	Other services	6.94	8.99	8.26	11.80
	TERTIARY	9.35	19.76	10.84	23.32
	ALL	100.00	100.00	100.00	100.00

Source : Registrar General, India, Census of India 1991, Final Population Totals, Paper 2 of 1992.

The data demonstrates that during 1981 census the female percentage was 0.87 which has declined to 0.66 percent during 1991. This decline in female participation in construction sector may be due to fiscal orientation policy of the government. To elaborate the point, most of the construction activities of the central government or public sectors are undertaken generally in far off places in urban areas to which the male numbers migrate to participate in such activities. The female generally participate in nearby town areas or places near to their villages as they bear more burden of domestic activities alongwith supplementing the income of the family. However, if we notice the table-1, item no. ix clearly shows that the percentage of women working "other services has increased from 6.94 per cent in 1981 to 8.26 per cent in 1991 census

This "other services" include domestic works, maid servants and services which the female members can perform near their home site. This increase in percentage of women participation in service sector may be due to migration of male members to urban areas in search of employment, off-farm activities and increased participation of male members in construction activities. This apparant from the table-1. The percentage of male participation in construction sector has increased from 1.87 to 2.32 during 1981-1991 census period.

Description of Construction Workers in the Early 20th Century

Royal Commission on labour which was instituted "to inquire into and report on the existing conditions of labour in industrial undertakings and plantations in British India; on the health, efficiency and standards of living of the workers and on the relations between the employers and the employed and to make recommendations" enquired into the conditions of construction labour employed as casual and contract labour in the construction of railways.

The number of workers employed as contract labour were not known by then. There were no provisions for housing, water supply, and sanitation for contract labour. Fair-wages clause did not exist in public contract. The introduction of contract system was found to be the most suitable arrangement for the British which neither wanted to manage the labour process nor be held responsible for the labour force.

Organisation of the Industry

Economic organisation of construction industry and various types of labour conglomeration for construction activities may broadly be classified as public and private sectors.

In public sector the constructions are undertaken by various departments and authorities of central and state government like public works department CPWD, posts and telegraphs, HUDCO etc. The construction activities include in its purview roads, bridges, official quarters commercial buildings, houses etc.

Based on investments, the construction activities can be

categorised as big, medium and small constructions.

In both public and private sectors, irrespective of size of constructions, the construction industry operates through a system of subcontract which varies depending upon size of construction and sector. The principal employers as well as constructors do not directly involve themselves in organising the labour process both in public and private sectors.

The contract system with its origin in the colonial period has provided a working method as well as an attitude in the public sector such that the departments have no responsibility towards labour or quality of construction. Thus, the exploitative system of construction works continued for centuries.

The written contracts however is accompanied by conditions most of which harp on quality. The principal employer provides cement and steel while the contractor would procure other construction materials. The work is carried out through subcontract. The conditions of contract stipulate that 10% of the bill could be withheld from payment for a period of time, in order to ascertain the quality of construction. Of course, such cases arise only in case of big constructions of public sector projects.

Similarly there are conditions for contract with respect to labour (apart from the plethora of labour laws which hold both the principal employer and contractor liable). It has been observed that the conditions relating to labour were violated in all work sites in both public sector and constructions in our case study.

In public works department though there are provisions for inspection, withholding of payments by the principal employer in cases of violations of contract conditions, there has never been cases of such action against contractors in spite of blatant violations of contract conditions. The contractors in the private sector has generally not taken labour licence to engage contract labour.

Subcontracting and Types of Recruitment ; General Scenario

In small constructions in the private sector, masonary, carpentry, painting, mosaic work etc were given on piece rate labour contract to maistris. Maistris, who are skilled workers, would bring their groups of skilled and unskilled workers to whom they had to pay time-rated wages. The construction materials would be provided by the owner and the maistry would organise the work, recruit the required number of workers and complete the task. This is the mode of construction, wherein the artisan organises the labour process. For concerting and earthwork either specialised groups would be engaged or the head mason would get additional hands recruited from the market place to carry out the work. Relationship between employer and workers exists for short durations, at most till a particular phase of construction lasts.

In the big and medium sized construction under the contract system, the contractors would provide construction materials but do not organise the labour process. They engage subcontractors who would recruit labour, carry out and supervise the work.

The big sites had more concreting and earthwork. Therefore, concreting groups were employed. The contractors had brought groups of labourers from rural areas, housed them on site, paid them low wages in order to maximise profits. Such labourers are generally recruited from drought-prone tribal villages of Orissa.

Even in big constructions where labourers are employed by contractors or builders for long duration, it is the subcontractors who organise and supervise the work. There is no direct relation between employer and labourers. Thus, the employer is not responsible for the work of the labourers. The labourers are paid distressed wages, discriminated, exploitated in the distant lands by the dadan subcontractors.

The terms of contract between contractor and subcontractor and between subcontractor and labourer are oral. Even when a small houseowner recruits labour directly from market place, only an oral contract exists.

Thus, the system of subcontract and temporary nature of work have resulted in the recruitment of thousands of construction labourers on subcontract and casual basis. There are the principal employers with massive capital outlay at one end of the complex chain of hierarchical relationships and lakhs of construction workers with highly insecure subsistence living standards on the other end. In between lies a whole hierarchy of intermediaries, contractors and subcontractors so that there is no link between employer and labourers. The invisibility of the labourers, and specifically, of the women labour has left the women to work in this industry with terms of employment, type of work, housing and living conditions determined by the nature of recruitment.

Types of Recruitment

Since contracting, subcontracting and labour contract were the methods by which construction was carried out in the public and private sectors, there was no difference with regard to recruitment modes between public and private sectors. But the recruitment of labour differed according to size of construction, big medium or small.

There are broadly three types of recruitment :

(i) Workers directly recruited by contractor and housed in the site.

(ii) Workers recruited from rural areas by subcontractors or labour contractors on certain norms and conditions by advancing loans known as dadan labourers.

(iii) Workers recruited from City Slums or Pavements market places by principal employers or maistris.

In the big construction sites the first and second types of recruitment were the most prevalent. There were women recruited by contractors retained on muster roll for long number of years but kept as temporary hands. They were housed on sites and kept moving from they need more hands at work for a few days, depend on the market place labour.

Objectives of the Study

(i) The study aims at analysing the history, organisation nature and working of construction sector in our country.

(ii) The study examines the socio-economic conditions of women construction labourers, with special reference to Orissa.

Methodology

Keeping the objectives in view it was decided to collect data from construction site from women labourers during their off time. Data relating to socio-economic variable like terms and conditions of work, nature of work, wage rate, wage discrimination, provision of health care, security measures etc. have been collected with the help of a questionnaire.

For collection of data two construction sites one from Uttar Pradesh Bridge construction employed labourers for Rushikulya Bridge construction near Aska, another at Berhampur, Neelanchala Housing Complex area construction labourers have been purpositively selected in view of easy illegibility. The first one Aska area belongs to public sector employed labourers and the second one belongs to private sector employed labourers. Twenty women labourers in Aska Rushikulya Bridge construction area and twenty women labourers in Berhampur Neelanchal Housing Construction have been randomly selected for the purpose of present study.

The data so collected with the help of questionnaire, interviews, observations and field notes by visiting several rounds to the sites have been used for the purpose of analysis.

Working and Living Condition

In the earlier paragraphs we have witnessed that construction work in Orissa, is being carried out by a system of contract and labour contract in public as well as private sectors. Therefore, both these sector have similar working conditions as well as insecurity of employment for the labour. However, for the labour, the conditions of work and living standard vary with respect to size of construction and types of labour recruitment.

Relations and Terms of Employment in According to Size of Construction

There is no direct employer-employee relation for most of the labourers. Only the directly recruited labourers of contractors employed by houseowners for small repair works, had a direct relationship with their employers.

In small repair works this relationship continues for a few days a week. In such cases number of workers are meagre. In general however, most of the labourers are recruited by labour subcontractors and labourers have no direct relation with employers. Since the maistries recruited the labour, supervised the work and made wage payments, the labourers consider them to be the actual employers. Thus, not only is the labour invisible to the employers but the employers are also invisible to labourers since subcontractors determine the conditions of employment according to the convenience of the contractors.

Nature of Works Performed by Women Labourers

In earth work, the men dig the foundation holes and fill the baskets with mud using spades, while women carry the earth and deposit them in the place alloted for it. Even though normally digging is done by male hands, it is not uncommon to find women handling crowbar and spade in earth work.

Masonary work involves construction of walls with brick and mortar and smoothing the surface of the walls, floor and roof as soon as the cement is applied. While both men and women prepare the mortar, women carry the bricks, mortar and water to the place where the mason is at work. She also assists mason in his work.

Curing work is mostly undertaken by women. As soon as concreting is over, the floors, roofs and walls have to be continuously wet with water. The water is allowed to stand on the floor in order that the mortar and cement would settle and dry properly. Curing has to be continued for a period of 10 days.

Breaking jalli is done by women. The bricks have to be broken into small pieces using a hammer, for laying the floor.

Concreting work involves both men and women. The materials required for concrete mixture is usually assembled near the machine by men, if this involves carrying bags of cement or sand. After the mixture is made, men and women form a human chain all along the scaffolding until the spot where jalli has to be deposited. In quick succession the bondli full of mixture is passed from one hand to another, and the work goes on the whole day as jalli work has to be completed within a single day.

In big sites more women are employed to do only concreting work while in small sites most women do combination of all types of works like carrying cement, water, sand, brick etc.

Quantum of Work

An attempt has been made at estimating the quantum and intensity of work done by female workers in certain areas of construction work. We tried to measure it in a period of five minutes for different types of work done by women, namely masonary, concreting, curing and earth work.

- In concerting where the bondlies of concrete mixture is passed from one hand to another, it was found that 40 bondlies passed through the hands of a women in 10 minutes.
- For masonry work, the women was found carrying 10 to 12 wet bricks on her head and sometimes climbing the scaffolding with the load on her head with great skill and grace. Each wet brick weighed about 2 Kg.

In curing she was found carrying water in a pot 10 times in an hour and pouring the water each time over the concrete structures. Each pot weighed 7 Kgs.

As every where else in the construction work too there exists the division of work between men and women in the 'unskilled' jobs. Although jobs such as balancing 12 bricks on the head while climbing the ladder and passing the bondlis of mixture along the heights in quick succession, require dexterity and skill along with great stamina and yet they are termed 'unskilled' jobs by everyone concerned. In this division of labour that had been described above, men and women are paid differently by the subcontractor. Wherever division of labour exists, no matter what work women do, the value of the work is considered less than that of a male labourer. This wage differentials become even more glaring where they do the same job such as concreting, and still get paid less than their male counter parts. Notwithstanding the fact that women do all the various types of work in many instances, women are always considered to be the lowest in the hierarchy of the system of subcontract and therefore paid the lowest in construction work.

Wage Rates and Number of Days of Work

The wage rates are lowest for women labour in all construction sites. The wage rates bore an inverse relation to regularity of employment and thus to the size of construction in Berhampur City. The daily wage rates of women varied from Rs. 20 to Rs. 22. In the big sites the workers were paid the least while they were assured of continuous employment for 20 - 22 days a month. In the small sector the market place women were paid the statutory Minimum of Rs. 25/- but the number of days of employment was less than 14. In the big constructions including the public sector sites, minimum wages were violated with impunity. Work experience is not taken into account in fixing wage rates. Thus, a woman with long years of experience is paid the same wage as a novice. Interviews among women labourers revealed the aforesaid facts.

Wage Differential Between Men and Women

In masonary the work done by men and women were similar but had difference. The men would bring cement bags, prepare the mix and put it in the bondli. The woman carries bricks, stones, cement mortar, and supply them for use in the construction works. While at an average male labourers receive Rs. 25 per day in private works, females receive only Rs. 20/-. In the event of accidents, sickness or during maternity, workers had to forego employment and wages. They got indebted during these periods either to moneylenders or neighbours (in small sites and market places) or to subcontractors (in big sites and among maistri attached labour). Mostly the rural labourers of Ganjam and Puri are indebted to labour contractors. Such labourers are known as dadan labourers who are employed outside the state and exploited by labour contractors.

Mode of Payment

Usually, the subcontractors and maistris received payment in piece-rate while labourers were paid on day rate. As the maistries were responsible for recruitment of workers, supervision and disbursement of wages, they were able to secure more money by inflating on record the number of workers under them.

Facilities

The construction labourers are provided with practically no amenities not even the basic amenities such as wholesome drinking water, toilets and urinals. Provision of these as well as canteens restrooms and creches are mandatory according to Contract Labour Regulation Act. The Act states that if contractor fails to provide amenities, the Principal employer can provide them and recover the cost from the contractor. But not only in two construction sites like Aska, U.P. Bridge Corporation and Neelanchala Construction area, all these were conspicuously absent.

It was only in Rushikulya Bridge construction site that drinking water was kept in pots at convenient places. On every other site workers had to look for water and walk some distance to reach it. Lack of toilets on the sites put women to a great deal of inconvenience.

Health Care

The women often complained of neck pain, chest pain, head-ache, body ache and fever, exhaustion and problems arising out of carrying wet construction materials on their heads. In big sites where there was continuous employment, they were compelled to rest for a few days every fortnight to recoup their energies. In general, no medical facility was provided by the employers and the labourers were compelled to spend money for medical care. Visits to hospitals meant that the labourers had to forego their work as well as wages for the day.

Maternity and Child Care

Women do heavy manual work even till the day of delivery. About 40% of the children born to these construction women were delivered by neighbouring women or relatives or by traditional midwives. During the first delivery most women stayed at home upto one year before returning to work. From the next delivery onwards they stayed for a period ranging from one month to three months.

Again because the industry did not compensate the women for loss of her earnings, she become indebted either to subcontractors or to money lenders. In big sites it was found that when a women was to deliver, the husband too stayed away from work in order to look after the wife. As they had to take loans from the subcontractors they were compelled to join work at the earliest with a view to repayment of loan.

In our analysis, 30 per cent of the women carried the children to the work site, 20% left them on their own at home, 25% left the infants in the care of elder girls or persons, 15% are sent to schools, 10% are employed in shops and commercial establishments.

Children on the site were exposed to the health hazards children were grossly neglected in the work site. Some times they quarrel themselves and sometimes play among themselves. Children were seen playing in the cement water, sands etc. Thus the total lack of child care facility seemed to affect the lives of the children of women labour in this sector.

Occupational Hazards and Accidents

The risk involved in construction work is very high particularly for women workers, who have to climb great heights carrying heavy loads. Accidents involving simple injuries occur every day while fatal accidents are not uncommon. Falling from heights, electric shock, falling of objects, and collapse of ladder, are the major reasons for fatal accidents, as revealed from interviews and field notes.

Long hours of work involving continuous handling of cement lime or other corrossive construction materials lead to the feet and hands being bruished burnt and eaten away. Women workers who carry the cement mix and wet bricks on their heads suffer serious problems like head-ache and fever. Pregnant women who carry heavy loads run a high risk of abortion.

There are no rules for safety in construction. Most of the women labourers have belonged to the landless agricultural labourers and migrants. In Neelanchal Housing Complex, women labourers mainly from Lochapada, Bhabinipur, Khodasing, Lanjipalli have revealed that they visit to their work in little family groups. After their return, they have to prepare food for the family members.

Similarly, in Rushikulya Bridge construction, women labourers of Ghatakuri, Baragam, Mukundapur, Babanpur, Nuagam also revealed the similar facts of work burden both at work site and at home. Thus, women labourers are doubly exploited and over burdened.

Socio-Economic Profile

The marital status of women labourers demonstrate that 60% of women were married, 12% were either widowed or divorced, 28% were unmarried women.

The interview revealed that in private construction works, the supervision is very serious and pressure of works are serious.

The Government sector exhibits low pressure of works. But the contractor who collect labourers take Re. 1/- from each women labourers as commission. About 40% of women labourers are totally illiterate among the women labourers.

Ignorance, tradition-bound attitudes, lack of skill, seasonal nature of employment, heavy physical work, lack of job security, long hours of work, lack of minimum facilities at the work place, ill-treatment and bondage are some of the features of the employment of women in construction sectors.

Policy Thrust

The foregoing analysis brought to light that most of evils in the construction industry have been directly attributed to the system of subcontract.

Government policy and labour laws should be more vigoriously directed towards ameliorating the living conditions of these vulnerable sections of the society especially women labourers who belong to the category of scheduled under privileged sections.

In view of these considerations, the following suggestions have been forwarded:

(i) Equal pay for all types of unskilled work and schemes for skilled upgradation for women should be undertaken, through strong endorcement of laws.

(ii) Provisions of housing and creche facilities must be ensured to women on all sites.

(iii) Existing laws should be amended to provide powers in inspection and prosecution and protection from victimisation.

(iv) Violation of laws by the contractor should result in cancellation of licenses and increased penalty.

(v) Hours of work for construction labour should be restricted to six hours, from early morning till noon. Safety norms should be evolved and enacted as a law. Women labourers should be provided toilet, drinking water and other minimum facilities.

(vi) When fatal accidents occur, it should be made mandatory for the principal employer to inform authorities and deposit the compensation before the labour commissioner.

(vii) Unless agricultural women labourers are educated, organised conceived regarding their rights awakened, they cannot be emancipated from socio-economic bondage.

(viii) A legal literacy programme can enable women labourers to apply that critical awareness to the law and legal process, discovering both the limits and possibilities of law in the battle for socio-economic change.

(ix) The construction women labourers being casual workers, are unable to claim subsistence allowance. In times of financial crises, they borrow at an exorbitant rate of interest leading to indebtedness. Hence, there should be adequate social security safety-nets alongwith their proper enforcement.

(x) As women labourers are doing monotonous, strenous back breaking work in unhealthy working conditions, they should be provided with protective equipments for handling the construction materials.

(xi) Such women construction labourers should be organised for uplifting their standards of living.

10

Socio-Economic Profile of Fisher-Women Community of Krushna Prasad Block (Orissa)

*Dr. S.N. Tripathy**
&
*Sri P.K. Patnaik***

An attempt has been made in this paper to highlight the Socio-economic problems of Fisherwomen Community of Biripadar village located in Krushnaprasad block in Chilika area of Puri district, (Orissa).

Objective of the Study

This study has been undertaken with the following objectives :

(i) To understand the Socio-economic conditions of the people depending on Chilika for earning their livelihood.

(ii) To assess the resources available in and around the lake.

(iii) To examine the efforts made by the community in bringing about socio-economic change, especially the women.

In India, a high proportion of working women are employed in the unorganised or informal sector; mainly in agriculture, livestock, forestry, fishing etc.; the percentage being 81 as per 1991 census.

* Sr. Lecturer in Economics, Aska Science College, Aska.
** Lecturer in Economics, K.D. Science College, Pochilima.

As per 1981 census, about 90 percent of women labourers employed in unorganised sectors which do not provide fair wages and good living standards. No supportive service like creches, fuel or water are available to such vulnerable section of the society.

The latest ILO report remarks, "All women are working women".

In most of the countries, the female workforce will be half of the total workforce by 2000 A.D. The ILO is concerned about the massive entry of women into active economic life without a corresponding improvement in their living standards. Over 60 per cent of Indian women over 7 years of age are illiterate compared with 35 per cent of Indian males.

The Human Development Report (HDR) 1995 has also brought to light that, "the monetization of non-market work of women is more than a question of justice. It concerns the economic status of women in society. Women's work were properly valued, it is quite possible that women would emerge in most societies as main breadwinners - or atleast equal breadwinners - since they put in more hours of work than men".

Another vital point brought to light was, that women carry 53 per cent and men 47 per cent of the total burden of work in developing countries. The ILO report aptly remarked, "the entry of women into the labour market permitted the majority of households, to cope with the reduction in real incomes provoked by the economic crises".

The Setting

The present study concerning the issues relating to problems and living standards of scheduled caste fishing community of Biripadar village. In India, as per 1991 census, the scheduled castes constitute 16.48 per cent who are economically the most deprived sections in the society.

The irony is that these scheduled caste fisher women suffered double oppression and exploitation because of low wages and labour discrimination. Pre-market discrimination exists when one group does not have access to these factors like education, skill, training etc., which improve human capital and enhance their marginal product. Post-market discrimination exists when individuals having similar amounts of human capital receive dispoportionate wages for their labour. Because of low opportunity cost of women, on the basis of socially available alternative uses of their time, they accept low wages, distressed working conditions and tedious works.

The plight of unorganised women labourers has been demonstrated due to their double burden of manual labour and maternal roles. Women are considered as "second class citizens" cannot participate in decision-making in any affair of the state. Women have to cook, grind grain, carry water on their back, gather wood, help their men flock in the fields, raise children etc.

Being perfurbed by their miserable economic conditions, a Pioneering attempt was made in 1992 to awaken the fishing community of Biripadar by United Artistic Association, Ganjam. For the purpose of present study primary data was collected by Sri Patnaik, one of the paper writers, with the help of a questionnaire.

Methodology

Keeping the objectives in view, the following methodology has been adopted.

- Village meetings/discussion with the local people pertaining to prevailing situation.
- Dialogue with individuals belonging to different categories of people and age groups.
- Contacts/discussions with the village level organisation, such as youth clubs, village libraries, women organisations and village committees.

In order to make an indepth study of various households the households have been grouped into four categories on the basis of their income level. The lowest income group (A) has the annual income level ranging from Rs. 2500/- to Rs. 5000/- with a total of 16 households.

Group B category consists of 42 household with an annual income level of Rs. 5001/- to Rs. 10,000/-. Group C and Group D have 13 and 4 households respectively with the income level of Rs. 10,000 to Rs. 15,000/ and above Rs. 15,000/-. Data were collected through interviews with the help of questionnaire.

Thus, on the whole, observational and interview methods have been adopted to find out facts.

Village survey is of paramount significance as it focuses light on various issues relating to living conditions of the community and their socio-cultural aspects. The findings of the survey would be certainly useful for evolving the formulation and implementation of development policy, plan or programme at the regional level.

Profile of the Village

Biripadar is a small fisherman community in the Chilika, Asia, largest brackish water lagoon of Krushnaprasad Block in Puri district. The village is inhibited by 75 fishermen families with a population, approximately 400. The rate of literacy is about 42%. The people of the village belongs to the Schedule Caste community known as 'Kandaras'. They earn their daily livelihood depending on Chilika lake.

Lack of communication is one of the hindrances to their development. Boat is the only means of communication from their village to the hinterland where as the state capital Bhubaneswar is at a distance of 130 kms. The district headquarter Puri is only at a distance of 58 kms. The Block Development Officer, Bank, hospital, college, school, are situated at a distance of 10 kms from the village. The village has a primary school with education facility upto 5th class. It is observed from the household survey despite the fact that there is a vast scope for utilisation of resources. The households are in the grip of ignorance and poverty due to low per capita income, lack of purchasing power, lack of communication, ill health and indebtedness.

The Government/Non-Government Organisations through its discussional welfare programmes can play an important role in bringing about socio-economic aspects of the people by providing ample avenues of resources utilisation.

Demographic Features

1. *Total Population, Sex Ratio, Age Composition*

An analysis of population, age, composition are of vital importance for studying the future trends of population growth, level of literacy and sex composition.

TABLE - 1

Groupwise Presentation of Population with Age Group.

Population (Group-wise)

Sl. No	*Age group*	*Male*	*Female*	*Total*	*% of Grand Total*
1.	(0 - 5) years	56	47	103	26.34
2.	(5 - 10) years	23	32	55	14.08
3.	(11 - 15) years	18	23	41	10.48
4.	(16 - 20) years	12	08	20	5.11
5.	(21 - 15) years	07	24	31	7.92
6.	(26 - 30) years	11	21	32	8.18
7.	(31 - 35) years	20	17	37	9.46
8.	Above 35 years	38	34	72	18.41
	Total	185	206	391	99.96
		(47.3%)	(52.7%)		

The total population of the 75 households stood at 391 as per Table - 1. The sex-wise distribution of population from Table - 1 reveals that there are about 47% males and 52% females. The population belonging to the age group of (0-5) is about 26% where as the population on under the age group of (5-10) years is about 14%. Thus, about 40% of the population face in the age group of below 10 years, under the age group of (11-15) and (16-20) years, there are population of 10% and 5%

respectively. Population under the age group of (21-25) years comes to 7%, where as the population under the age group of (25-30) years comes to 8%. In the age group of 31-35 and above 35 years there population of 9% and 18% respectively.

TABLE - 2

Literacy
Group-wise Presentation of Literacy Rate.

Group	*Total population*	*Male*	*Female*	*Children*	*Total*	*Group %*
A	70	11	02	08	21	30.8%
B	218	33	12	55	100	44.5%
C	65	12	03	21	36	50.7%
D	28	03	02	04	09	31.1%
Total	381	59	19	88	166	42.75%

Out of a total population of 391 persons of 75 households 166 persons are found literate which comes to 42.75%. The percentage of literate among males above 18 years constitute 69.4% where as the children in the age group of below 15 years constitutes 41.7% and females above 18 years constitute only 20%. The highest percentage of 50.7% of literacy is manifested in group C followed by group B with 44.6%, 32.1% in group D 30.8% in group A. It is evident from the analysis that Group A, Group D and Group B lag behind the average level of literacy 35.87%. On the contrary Group A exceeds the average literacy level.

Income

In every economic behaviour the level of income constitute important indicator of standard of living of the community, socio-economic status and pattern of expenditure. The source of income varies from person to person. The households derive their income various sources like Chilika (lake) fishing, fish and prawn business, seasonal manual labour etc. The impirical analysis of annual income of 75 households of fisherfolk families made through the Table - 3

TABLE - 3
Annual Income

Group	*Total Income from fish catching*	*No. of D.E.M*	*Const. of D.E.M*	*Sale of fish*	*Capital Investment (in Rs)*	*Non on Business*	*Annual income of the Group(in Rs.)*
A	67,000	02	3,600	-	30,000	4,000	75,100
B	2,62,800	12	28,700	1,000	2,51,000	19,600	2,92,500
C	1,13,900	05	15,000	1,300	1,32,000	28,200	1,13,200
D	49,800	03	15,900	25,900	31,000	-	91,600
TOTAL	4,91,000	22	63,200	28,200	4,44,000	51,800	5,89,400

The average annual income of household families worked out at Rs. 7754/-, which the income per day for each household is estimated at about Rs. 22/- only, the average monthly income for each household comes to Rs. 682/- only.

The total annual income of the 75 household families stood at Rs. 5,81,550/- only. However, the group average total annual income is found to be very low. It has been depicted that Group A, Group B, Group C, Group D have the annual total income of Rs. 4,731, Rs. 6,827/-, Rs. 11030/- and Rs. 18,928/- respectively.

It is revealed from the Table - 3 that, P.C.A.I. of the households in Group D and Group C are comparatively higher than Group B and Group A. This is due to the fact that Group D and Group C owned the capital assets, and equipments like nets, boats etc. for income generation. The lowest P.C.A.I. is Rs. 4,731/- found among the Group A households which presents their deplorable economic condition as they face below the poverty line.

Income from conventional sources (from fish catching and fish selling) constitute 84.77% of the total annual income of 75 households. Where as income from Non-conventional sources (i.e. from wage earning and other business except fish) constitute only 15.4% of the total annual income of the above mentioned number of households.

The study reveals that among the total household income contribution of other earning members towards household income constitute 10.86% of the total annual income. It is observed that the major impending Factors which obstruct their income generation are lack of adequate capital investment such as nets, boats, low work participation of the other earning members in economic activities like fishing and manual works.

Income From Conventional Sources

The total income from fishing of 75 households are Rs. 4,93,000/-. It is evident from the above table that the households of Group D has the highest total income from fishing which comes to Rs. 49,200/-. This ultimately reveals the fact that the households of Group D have higher productivity efficiency and they possess greater division of labour (i.e specialisation in the occupation) than that of the other groups and they are regular fishermen.

Fishing Equipments

Fishing requires a variety of equipments like different kinds of crafts and nets used in different seasons for catching fishes. Poverty, destitution, indebtedness combindly made in-roads to almost more than sixty per cent of the households claiming their prospects of modern methods in fishing and fish equipments.

The average value of fishing equipments of households works out at Rs. 5,920/-.

It is interesting to note that the average value of fishing equipment is higher in case of Group C (Rs. 10,153/-) compared to Group D (Rs. 7,750/-). Group A has the lowest average value of fishing equipment i.e Rs. 1,875/- followed by Group B with average value of fishing equipment Rs. 5,975/-. The total value of fishing equipment Group-wise reveals the following amounts Group A - Rs. 30,000/-, Group B - 2,51,000/-, Group C - Rs. 32,000/- and Group D - Rs. 15,000/-.

Ten out of 75 households constituting nearby 15% of the total households are having no fishing equipments. As a result these households work as wage labourers under the owners of fishing equipments with megre wages. These households are in the miserable condition of living due to lack of fishing equipments, and they assured source of employment as they are unemployed about 5 months in a year.

A study of the average household investment on fishing equipments and the income which it generates alongwith and income earned by family members through normal works come to an average income of Rs. 22/- per day which is extremely low. The meagre amount of Rs. 22/- represent the outcome of return on capital and wage of family labour.

It is found that because of inadequate capital equipment and their investment the income is very low.

Hence, it is suggested that urgent action is called for the provision of improved fishing equipments together with soft loan facility. Credit should be rationalised and should reach the households who urgently need for it productive investment.

A comparative study of total capital investment and the annual income generated out of it, from fishing of 4 groups has been made in the Table - 4.

TABLE - 4

Fishing Equipments
Income and Productivity of Investments (in Rs.)

Group	*Value of fishing equipment/ household*	*Annual income of Groups from fishing*	*Annual Y of OEM from fishing*	*Total Annual Y of Groups from fishing*	*Annual Y household from fishing*	*Capital output ratio*
A	1,875	67,100	3,600	68,700	4,293	43.67
B	5,955	2,62,800	9,400	2,72,00	6,480	91.89
C	10,153	1,13,900	11,000	1,24,900	9,607	105.68
D	7,750	25,800	13,500	39,300	13,100	59.16

The table reveals that capital output ratio is highest in case of Group C which is 105.68% followed by Group B with 91.89% Group A has the lowest capital output ratio of 43.67% followed by Group D with 59.16. However, it is clear that capital output ratio through differs among the various groups but it is certainly very high due to the fact that prawn culture and their export provide a lucrative earnings to the households. But it may not continue permanently and would cause have in their living standard due to ecological and other factors.

The Pattern of Expenditure

The expenditure pattern of households some remarkable features. Liquor figures prominently in the item of their daily consumption. Except 10% of the households all most all other sample households addicted to alcohol and smoking. The expenditure on consumption of alcohol, wine, and other habits drain away a considerable portion of their income leading to a deplorable state of living.

TABLE - 5

Expenditure on Alcohol

Group	*Population*	*Annual Income*	*Expenditure on Alcohol*	*% of Income*
A	70	73,000	14,760	20.23
B	218	2,86,750	29,100	10.82
C	65	1,43,400	9,780	6.82
D	28	74,700	2,640	
TOTAL	381	5,78,150	56,280	9.73

The expenditure on alcohol is approximately Rs. 56,280/- constituting 9.73% of the total annual households income spent every year on this unproductive consumption. To repeat consumption of wine is the major factor of their miserable condition. It has far-reaching repercussion on health, income and a relevant cause for growing dis-contentment. The Table - 5 reveals that no positive co-relation is marked between level of income and the amount of money is spent on alcohol.

16 households spend 20.13% of their income, which is the highest percentage among the households. Group B having spend 10.82% of his total annual income on wine consumption. 13 households and Group D with 4 households spends 6.82% and 3.53% of their income on liquor consumption respectively. The total expenditure on alcohol by all the households is about 9.73% of the total income.

(b) Expenditure on Food

The main food items of the households comprises of rice, dry fish.

The table-6 shows that a sum of Rs. 5,42,350/- constituting 93.81% of total annual income is spend on food every year by the households.

TABLE - 6

Food (Expenditure)

Group	*population*	*Annually in Rs.*	*Expenditure on food*	*% of Income*	*% of total Exp. on food*
A	70	73,300	1,03,815	141.63	10.06
B	218	2,86,750	3,10,921	108.27	30.10
C	65	1,43,400	92,480	64.49	8.96
D	28	74,700	35,640	54.03	2.58
TOTAL	381	5,78,150	5,42,356	93.81	–

Even though a major portion of the income is spend on food. It is a state of affair, that diet lacks nutritious and other vitamins. High expenditure on food consumption also indicated their poverty condition as it leads to meagre savings.

Though it is generally believed that the family size and age composition influence the expenditure on food, it is interesting to note that low level of income and high expenditure on food over and above the income as is the case of group A leads to indebtedness. Group A spending Rs. 1,03,815/- over their total income of Rs. 73,300/- justify to the aforesaid fact. The percentage of expenditure on food is the lowest in Group D which comes to 54.03% followed by Group C with 64.49%.

The consumption expenditure on food in case of Group C also exceeds the annual income, the percentage being 108.27%.

Expenditure on Clothing

The average households wear dhoti, lungi and gamucha. The young members adopted modern colourful dresses. Like pants, shirts and etc.

TABLE - 7

Expenditure on Clothing

Group	*Population*	*Annual Income*	*Exp. on Clothing*	*% of Income*
A	70	73,000	15,700	21.41 %
B	218	2,86,750	50,200	17.50 %
C	65	1,43,400	17,000	11.85 %
D	28	74,700	6,500	9.12 %
TOTAL	381	5,78,150	89,400	15.46 %

It is observed from the households that the total expenditure of clothing table-7 is approximately Rs. 89,400/-. The figure for the average households stood at Rs. 1192/- only. The groupwise expenditure on clothing is given in the Table -7, which indicates, that the households of Group A and Group B spend 21.41% and 17.5% of their income on cloth which is much higher than the percentage of expenditure made on cloth by Group C and Group D i.e. 11.85% and 9.12% respectively.

TABLE - 8

Expenditure on Education

Group	*Total Population*	*No. of Education Members*	*Exp. on Education to the total Income*	*% of Exp. On Edu.*
A	70	21	2,200	3.0 %
B	218	100	10,900	3.8 %
C	65	36	3,400	2.37 %
D	28	9	2,400	0.03 %
TOTAL	381	166	18,900	1.83 %

There is high level of illiteracy among the households and 42.1% of the population are literate. Literacy ratio is explained in Table -. 2, which shows that 69.4% of males 20.1% of females and 41.70% of children are literate. It is clear that there is high female illiteracy (about 80%). There is high drop out of the children and more than 58.1% of them are illiterate. They supplement the family earning by working/ assisting in different works of the households. Abject poverty and lack of awareness regarding the value of education have caused impediment in their efforts to attend school.

The expenditure on education table-8 is about Rs. 18,900/- (Rupees 252/- per household) annually by the households to support the education of their children which seems very meagre. The member of literate members are only 166 (42.45%) out of 391. The total amount of expenditure on education stood at 3.24% of their total annual income.

In the household Group D is spend more amount which constitute 3.54% (Rs. 600/- per household). Whereas, in Group A spend which constitute 1.15% (Rs. 137/- per household) so group A is the lowest income group cannot afford on education expenditure. The college going student is only one. The School going student are about 7, the school and college being at a distance of 4 kms and 10 kms from village. The primary education facility in the village is only upto 5th standard.

Expenditure on Health

The expenditure on health among the household is low. The annual expenditure on health is about Rs. 1,05,035/- (Rs. 1400/- per household). Which constitute 10.18% of their total expenditure and 18.16% of their total income. A few household spend a lot of money towards their health, because some patients belong to cardiological cases.

The distance of the local P.H.C. centre is 12 km. from the village and the nearest dispensary is available. Which is 6 km distance from the village. There is no health centre except a few, major diseases like Faleria, Chest pain, Cold Fever, Scabies, Skin diseases have occur it.

Lack of sanitation, proper nourishment food, grabages dirty water in and around the village, salty water and air in free in around the village environment. The health awareness is not there. Because mother of household are illiterate. So, they can take proper care of child health.

Festival & Entertainment

The fisher-folk communities of the village believe in religion. The total expenditure on festival and entertainment of the 75 household stood at Rs. 31, 250/- (Rs. 416/-) per household. Which constitute 5.40% of their total annual income. Sometimes they spend lavishly in celebrating some festivals in the village. Which becomes a burden to every household. Because of pressuries their current expenditure. There is no facility for entertainment. So young group are going to nearby to see the movies. Where as, the womenfolk visit to their relatives, friends and temples etc.

Debt Burden

Indebtedness of the household is the crucial problem for their socio-economic development. The credit facility by the government agencies is grossly inadequate. The money lenders and indigenous bankers play a vital role in the supply of credit to the households.

Most of the fishermen are addicted to intoxicants. So they, spend a lot money towards wine, liquor etc., secondly they are not aware of the methods and usefulness of saving money for future.

Their miserable living conditions and economic necessity force them to mortgage their durable assets with the money lenders and fish traders. But they could not release their assets due to heavy burden of debt and finally accepts wage earning and their principle means of livelihood. Thus, they face the extreme poverty and indebtedness.

It has been observed that the money-lenders and fish traders charge exorbitant rate of interest to the loan. The loan is spent for consumption purposes like food, cloth repair of house. Besides, the households also incur loan amount for buying fishing equipments. Expenditure on social festivals and health adversely effect their economic position as they could not repay the loan because of their subsitence income and finally leading to indebtedness.

Causes of Indebtedness

The investigation has brought into light that loans financed by non-banking institutions like moneylenders, and fish traders is comparatively higher. The institutional sources like banks provide a meagre percentage of 3.49% of the total credit needs subsidised scheme which comes to Rs. 45,700/- (including subsidy) for the last 3 year. A total of 8 households, out of 75 has been financed by banks which comes to only 10.6%.

The moneylenders, fish traders encourage fisherman to borrow from them. The investigation reveals that among the non-institutional sources like, the moneylenders provide 26.87% of the credit requirements. Which constitute a sum of Rs. 1,12,400/-. The rate of interest is as high as 60% per annum. It is surprising to note that all most all the households are indebted to the moneylenders.

The fish traders also offer advances to the households on the condition to sell and surrender good quantity of fish and prawn at a reasonable price to the former. It is seen that 15.69% of the credit requirement constituting a sum of Rs. 70,900/- is provided by the fish merchants to the households.

Apart from the aforesaid sources of finance fisher folk also approch their relatives, friends, to meet their credit requirements. The table shows that 55.8% of the credit requirements, which constitute Rs. 2,49,500/- has been supplied by friends, relatives. The credit from this source is negligible with very low rate of interest or no interest. But the loan is to be paid back positively sooner or later. The total debt amount is Rs. 4,64,250/- at all the end thus, the average debt burden comes to Rs. 6,190/- per households.

The perusal of the study brings into light that the Group A incurred the highest debt that is Rs. 1,15,900/-. Next comes Group B with a debt burden of Rs. 1,68,850/- and Group C with debt of Rs. 1,13,400/-. Lastly the Group D with a heavy burden of Rs. 25,200/- comparatively a small amount. Because this Group belongs to higher income Group (Rs. 15,000 and above).

TABLE - 9

Extent Of Indebtedness

Group	*Total % Income*	*Total Debt*	*D/Y% 100*
A	73,300	1,59,000	158.11%
B	2,86,750	1,68,850	58.89%
C	1,43,900	1,34,300	93.65%
D	74,700	33,200	55.11%
TOTAL	5,78,150	4,51,750	78.14%

Y - Indicates - Income
D- Indicates - Debt

The Table - 9 shows that the magnitude of indebtedness of various groups. The figure estimated by the formula D\Y 100 in the order of higher to lower extent of indebtedness. The indebtedness of the groups are as follows: group A 158.11% group B 58.89% Group C 93.65% and Group D 51.11%.

Especially, the Group A is over burden and it incurs excess expenditure to their income. This Group belong to the lowest income group (Rs. 2,501 to 5,000).

Assets Position

Assets are crucial factors in enhancing the level of income and standard of living of a family. It generates income and sustains development. So a study of assets position has some relevance in this context.

House

House is the basic necessity of life. It is noticed that all the households are living in thatched houses. Due to their low income position they could not build pucca-houses. They follows the joint family system and live under one roof. The house is built by mud, bamboo, wood etc.

No households belonging to higher income groups reside in pucca houses. Some households are having additional houses and therefore 75 households are having 82 houses.

Other Assets (Group-wise)

In addition to having the households also possess different types of utensils, of traditional designs, but mainly they use stainless steal. The total value of the utensils stood at Rs. 1,17,700/- constituting 10.5% of the total assets. The value of the ornaments, gold is approximately constituting Rs. 1,38,300/- from their total assets. But, the agricultural land asset is very less about to say Rs. 21,250/- constituting 1.89% of their total assets.

The value of other assets like furnitures, fans, radios, tape recorders, watches, bicycle comes to Rs. 77,510/- which constitute 14% of their total assets.

Saving

Saving rate is very low in every household. The cause is low per capita income, extravagant use of intoxicants, ignorance of saving, indebtedness etc.

The problem of marketing, communication, transport, lack of specialisation of human capital, Banking and credit facilities are some of the bottlenecks in the socio-economic development of the community under review. The sea route is the only means for their communication, in this connection public agency can play a major role by entering into the market to purchase the excess supply during high productivity at a minimum price. The linkage of production with marketing through co-operative will immensely help to avoid the default of payment and eleminate the exploitation of middlemen and fish traders.

Modernising the equipment for better earning, adequate institutional finances to rescue the indebted headloads from the clutches of the moneylenders, supply of fishing equipments, along with spread of education will go a long way in ameliorating their socio-economic conditions.

Policy Implications of the Study

The foregoing analysis brought to light that the problem of the socio-economic condition of fisherfolk (Chilika) of Biripadar village under review.

It is the irony that despite 48 years of independence, plan efforts have not been successful in ameliorating the economic conditions of poor fisherwomen community of Biripadar village under review. The moneylenders and fish traders exploit the simple, illiterate households through multifarious ways. The distressed sale of fish and prawn to the fish traders cause a miserable living of the community. Imperfect market conditions, lack of infrastructure and transportation are the factors responsible for the extremely low income of the fisherwomen community.

In this study, fisherwomen constituting 52 percent where as males constituting 47 per cent (Table-1), literacy is as low Rs 20.1 per cent compared to male folk 69.4 percent (Table-2) represent the most distressed and deprived segment of the society. Fruits of planning and Governmental policy measures could not lift such depressed women from the grip of poverty and indebtedness. Hence, all steps should be undertaken to ameltiorate the living conditions of such poverty-striken fisherwomen community of Krushnaprasad block. An important point to be kept in view is that the subsistence fisherwomen labourers are prone to health hazards like diarrhoea, dysentery, cholera and fever. Several women and children die suddenly and unexpectedly without health care and proper nourishment. Hence, the immediate need of the hour is better provision of health care.

In this unorganised fishing industry the fisherwomen community suffer because of high degree of 'Casualism'. Therefore emancipation of fisherwomen community is indispensable for providing social justice to fisherwomen.

The socio-economic and cultural traditions have restrained fisherwomen from acquiring skills, modernised equipments, technology to suit themselves to the changing need of the time. Hence, it is suggested that the fisherwomen community should be imparted proper education, training, assets and equipments to strengthen their economic and social living standards.

11

Socio-Economic Issues and Women Legislators of Orissa : During British Period (1936-1947)

Dr. V. Rajendra Raju

This paper focuses light on the role of women legislators during Pre-independence era, for the emancipation of women in the state of Orissa.

Orissa became a separate province on 1st of April 1936. On the basis of Government of India Act 1935, elections to different stage legislators were held. Accordingly, election for the sixty member Orissa Assembly was held. Indian National Congress was the only prominent political party. It got 36 seats. Since Congress decided to remain away from ministry making on all Indian basis, a minority Government was installed in Orissa under the leadership of Maharaja Krushna Chandra Gajapati Narayan Deo of Paralakhemundi. This ministry was installed in April, 1937 and continued upto the last week of July, 1937 to make way for the formation of Congress Ministry under the Prime Ministership of Sri Biswanath Das. Announcement was also made that the first session of the Assembly would start from 28th July, 1937. The ministry remained in power till 4th November, 1939 and during this period of about two years and four months the ministry had to settle a number of social, economic and political problems faced by the province which had just been born and to implement the policies and programmes commited by the Congress Party during the elections. In this election Sarala Devi and A. Laxmibai were elected from Cuttack and Berhampur town respectively.

They were the first Oriya ladies elected representative in the Orissa Legislative Assembly. Their speeches as legislators reveal the fact that they not only bold and courageous but also were eager for the welfare of the women society and for the alround development of the state.

By that time about twenty per cent of the Hindu population belonged to the Scheduled Caste. They have been described as 'Avarna' or without Varna. For thousands of years they have left apart, worked apart, eaten apart and worshipped apart. Their touch was considered impure and was a source of pollution.

For the uplift of the Harijans and for preaching the message of removal of untouchability the Prime Minister in his first budget speech expressed the concern of the ministry towards Harijans and backward classes. He said, "It is our earnest desire that these classes, kept backward and depressed should have their due place in society and make their best contribution to the highest well-being of the country.[1]

In pursuance of the Government's policy outlined in the budget speech provisions were made for stipends, scholarships, remission of fees, free supply of books and slates and hostel facilities to the students of these classes. Grants of funds were also made to the schools for teaching Harijans and backward classes.[2]

Sarala Devi took keen interest for the development of Harijans. On 7th September, 1937 she put questions as to what the Government has done to extend suitable facilities to Harijans in the field of education and employment.[3] She compelled the Government to provide better education and employment to them in order to redress their financial difficulties.

Due to poverty the harijans were borrowing money with high interest from the money-lenders. During collection of debt, the money-lenders were sometimes applying criminal method to exact as much money as possible from the debtor without taking into account of debt.

Sarala Devi challenged the inhuman activities of the money-lenders and asked the Government to open Agriculture Bank and Land Mortgage Bank for these people including the poor farmers.[4]

In Ganjam district, most of the Harijans were employed as watchers in the reserve forest In 1938, some of them were removed from service all on sudden although they had put in services ranging from 10 to 20 years. When these people were thrown out of employment, Mrs. A. Laxmibai as a legislator asked the Government, 'why was such a drastic step taken by the forest department.[5] She criticised the Government bravely for this type of activities and appealed the government to give them employment urgently.

Due to the sincere efforts of Sarala Devi and S. Laxmibai, the Government of Orissa was forced to sanction funds for the building of Kaibalya Kutir, a hostel for Harijans at Cuttack.

Harijans of Sambalpur were allowed free to use forests for rearing cocoans. Subsidy were paid to the spinner's associations to encourage spinning and weaving among the pans of Angul. Circulars were issued to all Departments for appointment of local people with preference to Harijans and tribals in clerical and ministerial grades.[6]

Due to their sincere efforts the caste Hindus employed the Harijans, accepted food and water from them, wells and bathing ghats were opened for them and they were encouraged to participate in the public dinners. This process of socilisation and interaction made a great impact on both rural and urban life of Orissa.

Gandhiji was very much impressed by these type of activities of women in Orissa and desired that women in other places of India also should follow the foot steps of the Oriya ladies.

By that time the Judicial Court of Jeypore became regularly irregular for which the Court became over burdened with cases. So, the Bar Association of Jeypore put a memorandum to the Government stating their demand for permanent building of the Court and regularise its office.

Inspite of this letter from the Bar Association on 08.081937, the Government remained silent for months together. Tribals were deprived of socio-economic justice. At this juncture, A. Laxmibai took interest for the Jeypore people and placed it before the Assembly on 24th January, 1938. She drew the attention of the premier to this matter.[9] On the same day, she raised a number of questions on the issue of Forest Guards.

When the finance Minister of the first Congress ministry presented the budget in the Assembly at that time she was pleased to see the Budget and offered congratulations to the minister and his Cabinet.[10]

At the same time she suggested some steps to be taken to eradicate unemployment, improvement of Cottage Industry, development of paper industry, improvement of women education, abolition of fees for collection of wood from jungle,[11] and the establishment of Central Museum-Cum-Emporium at Delhi.

On the eve of Second World War, corrupt businessmen raised the market price by hoarding essential commodities and thereby, poor people suffered a lot. So for smooth distribution of essential commodities, Sarala Devi dragged the attention of the Government to open godown and Government stores in every district and sub-division. Moreover, in order to check the misutilisation of stock by the Government employees she stressed on the maintanance of stock registers regularly at the site.[12]

Due to her strong arguments, Government remained vigilant on the public works, specially in the smooth distribution of essential commodities.

Sarala Devi took interest for the development of female education[13] as a legislator. She putforth valid arguments on 28th February, 1939 in the Assembly in favour of co-education and more funds for the promotion of female education.[14]

Sarala Devi further demanded that as most of the village ladies were remaining in unhygienic condition and were not aware of sanitary system, lady sanitary inspectors and vaccinators should be employed.[15]

On 24th March, 1939 Orissa Legislative Assembly met in the Ravenshaw College Hall with Sarala Devi in the Speaker Chair. She started the business of the Assembly in Oriya language breaking for the first time the tradition of debate in English language in British India.[16]

Sarala Devi knew very well the importance of the role of a legislator in democratic country. When she noticed irregularitics in the attendance of some of the members in the house she raised a question in the debate.[17] She demanded the no payment of salaries and allowances to those who remain absent in the house.

Besides this she suggested measures for the development of Legislative Assembly by opening separate wings for law, commerce and labour departments of Orissa. She also argued for the development of Chandabali Port[18] and to take immediate steps to improve its condition.[19]

During this period, the age of marriage for girls was eight or nine, although it often differed in some castes or provinces. This practice was modified by Government Legislation i.e. the Child Marriage Restraint Act. However, the Bill provided only negligible protection.[20]

Sarala Devi realised its importance for the liberation of women. So, she again introduced it in the Legislative Assembly as "The Child Marriage Restraint Act (Orissa Amendment) Bill in 1938" in the house on 28th January, 1938.[21]

When Sarala Devi introduced this bill in the house some members who were conservative in nature opposed it. But after a long discussion, the Speaker announced "the Bill will have to pass in several stages. Nobody can prevent any member from contesting the principle of the Bill at any subsequent stage." Later on, the motion was adopted.[22]

Sarala Devi was in favour of abolition of the practice of dowry[23], and therefore, she introduced "The Orissa Dowry Abolition Bill, 1939," in the house on 15th September 1939 stating the urgent need of it.[24]

Entire house supported it and as a result the Bill was passed.[25]

The Congress ministry resigned from office on 4th November, 1939. The Government assumed direct responsibility for administration of the province. The Orissa Assembly was kept under suspension. During Quit India Movement, many Congress leaders were taken into custody. This led to the second minority coalition Government in Orissa under the leadership of the Maharaja of Paralakhemundi.[26] During this time

Sarala Devi introduced the Orissa Hindu Women's right to property Bill in the House. The motion was adopted.[27]

The ministry remained in power about twenty eight months. The Congress ministry did useful work in the field of tenancy reforms, Harijan upliftment, restoration of civil liberties, prohibition, and new education policy, etc. Being prominent legislators of that period, Sarala Devi and A. Laxmi Bai at different times, in different manner promoted courage and confidence among the people to pursue their struggle for Swaraj and complete independence.

After the World War-II, fresh election was held to the Orissa Assembly in early 1946. The Congress Party obtained 47 seats out of which for two seats, A. Laxmibai and Priyambada Devi were elected from Berhampur and Cuttack. This time also these women legislators took interest for the development of education and other works in the interest of the people and the province.[28]

Notes and References

1. O.L.A Proceedings, Vol. I, 1937, p. 55.
2. Government at work, 1937-38, p. 19.
3. Proceedings of the 1st Legislative Assembly of the Governor of Orissa, 1937, Vol. I, p. 263.
4. Proceedings of the First Legislative Assembly of the Governor of Orissa, 1937, Vol. I, p. 523.
5. Proceedings of the First Legislative Assembly of the Governor of Orissa, 1938, Vol. II, p. 34.
6. I.A.R, 1938, Vol. II, p. 215.
7. Samaj, 17 March, 1977.
8. Nabeen, 11 June, 1940.

9. "...... will the Government be pleased to state, whether Government have received a memorial signed by the member of the Bar Association, Jeypore dated 8th August, 1937 addressed to the Premier about the location and continuance of the court of the agency subordinate judge at Jeypore."

(Extract from O.L.A. Proceeding of 1938, Vol. II, No. 1, p. 25).

10. Mr. Speaker : Sir, "I congratulate the Hon'ble Finance Minister on the presentation of the Budget. I am glad that the Congress Government is trying to aim at giving greater happiness and contentment to the have nots in every shape and form. Thanks to the Prime Minister and his Cabinet......".

(Extract from O.L.A. Proceeding 1938, Vol. II, No. 15, dated 2 March, 1938, pp. 1053 to 1055).

11. O.L.A. Proceeding 1938, Vol. II, No. 15, pp. 1053 to 1055.

12. "...... will the Government be pleased to state whether there are public Works Department godown to stock Government stores in every district and sub-division.

Whether stock registers are regularly maintained and stock is periodically inspected by responsible officers.

Whether articles not required for immediate Government purpose are sold and if so at what intervals ?"

(Extract form the proceedings of O.L.A. Vol. II, No. 7, dtd. 1st February, 1938).

13. Though modern education had made a good deal of progress, people of Orissa were not in favour of giving education to women for enabling them to hold remunerative jobs like teaching. For most of people the women, educated or uneducated were meant to be only housewives. As a result there was a want of female teachers, which was a great hinderance to the spread of female education.

Review of Education in Bengal (1829-9 to 1896-97) 1st Quinquennial Report incorporated with Annual Report, 1896-97, Cuttack, 1897, p. 122.

14. Sir, I am for co-education. It is futile at present with rapid pace and co-education, is a thing which has been supported by many eminent public men and scholars of India and of other countries. The present meagre resources of Orissa requires that co-education are very few in number. So I am strongly supporting the basis of co-education in this province. So I am not very enamoured of this budget although framed by my party Government."

(Speech of Sarala Devi, extracted from the O.L.A. Proceedings, Vol. IV, No. 3 of dtd. 28th February, 1939).

15. O.L.A. Proceedings, Vol. IV, No. 3, dated the 28th February, 1939.

16. O.L.A. Proceedings, Vol. IV, No. 9, dated the 24th March, 1939.

17. "...... will the Government be pleased to state if they have made any rule under Section-5 of the O.L.A. members salaries and allowances Act 1938, defining the circumstances in which deduction from the salary of a member can be made, if not what other method there is for enforcing regular attendance of members at Assembly meetings."

    (Extract from the Proceedings of O.L.A., Vol. IV, No. 16 of dtd. 3rd April, 1939).

18. Chandbali is an important ancient port in the east coast of Orissa in Balasore district.

19. O.L.A. Proceedings, Vol. IV, No. 17, of dated 4th April, 1939.

20. Agnew Vijay, op. cit., pp. 18-20.

21. "Sir : I beg to move for leave to introduce a Bill to amend the Child Marriage Restraint Act in its application to the Province of Orissa".

    (Extract from O.L.A. Proceeding, Vol. II, No. 5 of dated the 28th January, 1938 p. 305.)

22. O.L.A. Proceeding, 1938, Vol. II, No. 5, p. 307.

23. Dowry is defined as the property, in cash or kind or both, women brings to her husband, or the property a man receives, when he marries either from his wife or her family.

24. "I beg to introduce the Orissa Dowry Abolition Bill, 1939. Sir, the importance of such a measure cannot be over estimated. It is a long felt need."

    (Extract from O.L.A. Proceedings 1939, Vol. V of dated 15th September, 1939, pp. 324-325).

25. O.L.A. Proceedings 1939, Vol. V, of dated the 15th February, 1939.

26. Orissa Review, Vol. XLIV, No. I, August 1987, p. 15.

27. O.L.A. Proceedings, 1942, Vol. VI, p. 207.

28. O.L.A. Proceedings, 1946, Vol. II, No. 9, pp. 295-296.